BENJAMIN FRANKLIN AND THE AMERICAN CHARACTER

Problems in American Civilization

UNDER THE EDITORIAL DIRECTION OF
George Rogers Taylor

PURITANISM IN EARLY AMERICA

THE CAUSES OF THE AMERICAN REVOLUTION

BENJAMIN FRANKLIN AND THE AMERICAN CHARACTER

THE DECLARATION OF INDEPENDENCE AND THE CONSTITUTION

HAMILTON AND THE NATIONAL DEBT

THE TURNER THESIS CONCERNING THE ROLE OF THE FRONTIER IN
AMERICAN HISTORY

THE GREAT TARIFF DEBATE, 1820–1830

JACKSON VERSUS BIDDLE — THE STRUGGLE OVER THE SECOND BANK OF
THE UNITED STATES

THE TRANSCENDENTALIST REVOLT AGAINST MATERIALISM

SLAVERY AS A CAUSE OF THE CIVIL WAR

RECONSTRUCTION IN THE SOUTH

DEMOCRACY AND THE GOSPEL OF WEALTH

JOHN D. ROCKEFELLER — ROBBER BARON OR INDUSTRIAL STATESMAN?

THE PULLMAN BOYCOTT OF 1894 — THE PROBLEM OF FEDERAL
INTERVENTION

WILLIAM JENNINGS BRYAN AND THE CAMPAIGN OF 1896

AMERICAN IMPERIALISM IN 1898

ROOSEVELT, WILSON, AND THE TRUSTS

PRAGMATISM AND AMERICAN CULTURE

THE NEW DEAL — REVOLUTION OR EVOLUTION?

FRANKLIN D. ROOSEVELT AND THE SUPREME COURT

PEARL HARBOR — ROOSEVELT AND THE COMING OF THE WAR

THE YALTA CONFERENCE

INDUSTRY-WIDE COLLECTIVE BARGAINING — PROMISE OR MENACE?

EDUCATION FOR DEMOCRACY — THE DEBATE OVER THE REPORT OF THE
PRESIDENT'S COMMISSION ON HIGHER EDUCATION

IMMIGRATION — AN AMERICAN DILEMMA

LOYALTY IN A DEMOCRATIC STATE

BENJAMIN FRANKLIN AND THE AMERICAN CHARACTER

EDITED WITH AN INTRODUCTION BY

Charles L. Sanford

Problems in American Civilization

READINGS SELECTED BY THE
DEPARTMENT OF AMERICAN STUDIES
AMHERST COLLEGE

D. C. HEATH AND COMPANY; Boston

INTRODUCTION

FOR better or worse, rightly or wrongly, Benjamin Franklin has been identified with the American national character. Though greater hero worship has been accorded to Washington and Lincoln, Americans and Europeans have judged Franklin to be more representative. They have called him "the first American," "the father of all the Yankees," "the multiple American." As a result, he has become a center of controversy, a conspicuous target for abuse by critics of American society and a rallying point for defenders of the American "way of life."

The problem presented here is a problem in values and in historical interpretation. Americans who read the promise of American life chiefly in terms of economic opportunity and technological advance hail Franklin as the patron saint of material success. For them the essential Franklin is the provincial hero and tinkerer of their schoolbooks. Critics of Franklin and the American society, for the most part, accept this portrait, but place a different evaluation upon it. They point out the grave defects of materialistic values. In the face of this criticism, the more recent defenders of Franklin and the American character, led by Carl Van Doren, author of the prize-winning biography (1938), have tended to discard the popular image of Franklin as being incomplete and inaccurate. They say that Americans have done Franklin and themselves a great injustice in making a parody of Franklin their guide through life. They see the problem primarily as one of his-

torical interpretation and maintain that the "real" Franklin which their research has uncovered is worthy of emulation and representative of the best traits in our society. The purpose of this volume is to present the best materials available from both sides of the case for and against Franklin and the American character so that the reader may come to his own conclusions.

Benjamin Franklin himself opens the volume as spokesman for the essential historical Franklin with selections from his *Autobiography*. The next group of readings early raises an issue pursued directly and indirectly throughout the volume: whether the attribute of "greatness," so frequently bestowed upon Franklin, is merited. During his lifetime Franklin achieved an almost universal celebrity, as the first selection, a letter by George Washington, attests. But another famous contemporary, John Adams, records a dissenting view. John Adams in the next selection admits Franklin's fame but argues that it is not wholly deserved because it owes a great deal to the excitability of public opinion in a revolutionary period, an excitability which, with Franklin's cooperation, made him a symbol of the great changes then taking place. The last selection in this group forms an introduction to modern interpretations of Franklin. Here Carl Van Doren exhumes and refutes John Adams' old argument, defending the view that Franklin would have been great in any age or place.

But Van Doren also uses the occasion

to reply, indirectly and with dignity, to all the modern detractors of Franklin who have tried to puncture what they consider the myth of his greatness. For critics of Franklin in the twentieth century, by writing in a mood of savage debunking after a long-entrenched convention of extravagant hero worship, have made a major issue of Franklin's greatness. Van Doren's confessed purpose in writing his monumental biography was to restore to Franklin his "magnificent central unity" and "rescue him from the dry, prim people" who made him an object of debunking. Whether the conscientious efforts of Van Doren and his more recent followers since World War II to document Franklin's claim to greatness indicate the emergence of a new pattern of hero worship is something which the reader must decide for himself.

The modern critics of Franklin and the American character are represented in the next group of readings. This group includes critical judgments resulting from sober, systematic analysis as well as the more passionate denunciations from the modern school of debunkers. Professor Frank Davidson, a Professor of English at the University of Indiana, opens the modern debate in this volume on a dignified note by projecting a problem in values for Americans. His essay, "Three Patterns of Living," contrasts the utilitarianism of Franklin unfavorably with the religious mysticism of his contemporary, Jonathan Edwards, and with the humanitarianism of John Woolman, another contemporary. The rest of the essays in this group of critical readings are concerned with defining the nature of the Franklin cultural tributary and exploring some of its more serious moral and spiritual consequences for Americans.

Modern criticism of Franklin has been greatly influenced by the work of a Ger-

man sociologist, Max Weber's *The Protestant Ethic and the Spirit of Capitalism* (published in 1920, but not translated into English until 1930). In it Weber used Franklin as exhibit number one to prove his thesis that Puritan asceticism, by inculcating thrift, sobriety, industry, and the sanctity of private property, had the very worldly consequence of promoting the rise of capitalism. Weber's approach made it possible to dismiss these virtues, and Franklin himself, as "bourgeois." Weber's point of view is represented in this volume by the next essay, A. Whitney Griswold's "Two Puritans on Prosperity." Griswold, a historian and now the President of Yale University, in this essay defines the main Franklin cultural tributary as the cult of material success. His picture of the essential historical Franklin thus agrees with the popular stereotype of Franklin as the hero of the capitalist success story, but places a different value upon it.

The next selection in the case against Franklin and the American character is by Gladys Meyer, a Columbia University scholar. Her findings tend to confirm those of A. Whitney Griswold, but she is more concerned with the urban pattern of success and its personal costs to Franklin as a human being, a friend, a husband, and a father.

With the last two contributors to the case against Franklin the tone of dignity in the debate becomes momentarily lost. The examination of the spiritual consequences of material success by the literary historian, Charles Angoff, supplements that of Gladys Meyer. But where Gladys Meyer discovers a redeeming quality in Franklin's wide tolerance, Charles Angoff sees only "miserliness, fanatical practicality, and lack of interest in what are usually known as spiritual things." His chief charge against Franklin is vulgarity in writing. The English novelist D. H. Lawrence in the last essay in this group scrutinizes the morality of capitalistic success. He condemns Franklin for a false and vicious moralism which mistakenly equates virtue with material goods and gadgets and which stifles honest, creative impulses through the pressures of social conformity. With Lawrence this side of the debate is brought to a fitting conclusion, because he combines his denunciation of what he regards as Franklin's narrow prudential morality with a wholesale attack on America.

The editor of this volume, Charles L. Sanford, opens the rebuttal by Franklin's defenders with his essay, "An American Pilgrim's Progress." In it he accepts the view of the critics that the success story and a related moralism are the essential ingredients of the historical Franklin, but argues that these reflect the American sense of mission and a faith in moral regeneration based on a poetic conception of the frontier.

The next selection reveals the main strategy of the Franklin defense, which is to emphasize other aspects of Franklin's life and character than the cult of material success. The humanist literary critic, Stuart P. Sherman, contends that Franklin, far from being the "lowbrow" pictured by Charles Angoff or simply the racy provincial hero of the success story, was actually one of the most widely and thoroughly cultivated men of his age. Sherman stresses the broad humanity of Franklin's political conceptions as opposed to political expediency and his affinity for theoretical science as opposed to the practical mechanic and gadgeteer. Although Sherman was writing in 1922 before the great debate began, his essay anticipates many of the views developed in greater detail in the more recent defences included here.

One of the earliest and best answers to D. H. Lawrence is that of Herbert Schneider, a pragmatist and Professor of Philosophy at Columbia University, whose defence of Franklin from his pioneering work, *The Puritan Mind* (1930), appears at this point. According to Schneider, a well-informed understanding of Franklin's philosophy and personal life would reveal that Franklin's table of virtues were not intended to be taken as a statement of the final ends of life, as D. H. Lawrence mistakenly supposed, but rather as instrumental virtues to be supplemented by other values, to which Franklin had an easy, spontaneous hospitality. Lawrence confused means with ends. Since the first appearance of Schneider's interpretation, a common retort to D. H. Lawrence has been that "this romantic, mystical Englishman" did not understand the characteristically American philosophy of pragmatism, of which Franklin was an early practitioner. Pragmatism, as expounded by William James, holds that ideas have no intrinsic value apart from experience and empirical test. Schneider therefore applauds Franklin for placing the Puritan frontier morality on a utilitarian footing and giving it empirical foundations.

The next selection by I. Bernard Cohen, a specialist in the history of science at Harvard University and long a student of Franklin's scientific activities, extends Schneider's point of view. Cohen maintains that "the empirical temper" provides the key to Franklin's character, explaining his approach to science, morals, and human affairs. But he argues that Franklin's most original contribution, insufficiently understood and appreciated by Americans, comes in the field of science, in which he ranks with Isaac Newton. Like Stuart Sherman and Carl Van Doren in the introductory essay, Cohen is concerned to expose the fallacies in the picture of the grubby-minded gadgeteer presented by Angoff and others.

The final indictment of Franklin in this volume, Angoff's charge of vulgarity in writing, is met in the concluding essay by Carl Van Doren, who, without mentioning Angoff by name, contends that Franklin was a great man of letters as well as a great scientist. The volume ends on the same note with which the controversy began, the theme of Franklin's greatness.

The conflicting opinions found in this volume admit of no easy solution. Who was the historical Franklin and what were his essential qualities? Upon answering this question, the reader must decide whether the basic elements of Franklin's character were primarily props for the economic order and a technological civilization, as the critics believe, or whether they tended to check and moderate the most materialistic aspects of our society, as the defense maintains.

The deeper, underlying issue, however, is whether the concept of nationality, or structure of values, embodied in Franklin forms an adequate basis for human relationships in our complex, modern world. Did Franklin find a satisfactory balance between individual enterprise and public enterprise? Can the example of Franklin help us to find the imagination, the sympathy, and the will necessary to control our vast technological machine for human ends? Is Franklin's vision of the good life for Americans broad enough to facilitate understanding between ourselves and other peoples? These questions are closely related to one another.

With respect to the last question there is a split within the readings which is not brought out into the open. On the one hand, such writers as Charles Sanford, Herbert Schneider, and I. Bernard Cohen regard Franklin primarily as a product of frontier conditions, while on the other Gladys Meyer and Stuart Sherman consider him the spokesman of an urban culture extending from Europe to colonial Boston and Philadelphia. The latter point of view reflects a growing concern, in the light of our international responsibilities, to understand our culture as an extension of Western European civilization rather than as something exclusive and unique. The essay by Stuart Sherman shows the possibility for mutual understanding and peace inherent in this conception of nationality. But if the frontier interpretation of Franklin's character is right, the essays by D. H. Lawrence and Charles Sanford will suggest the dangers to international understanding of self-righteous materialism or excessive national pride. Such a conclusion is not the inevitable consequence of a frontier interpretation, however, for the essays by I. Bernard Cohen and Herbert Schneider may suggest that frontier values are not incompatible with a broad cultural, humanitarian outlook.

[NOTE: The statement in the "Clash of Issues" on page xiii by Sydney G. Fisher is quoted from *The True Benjamin Franklin* (Philadelphia: J. B. Lippincott, 1899), p. 310; that by Gilbert Chinard from "Looking Westward" in *Meet Dr. Franklin* (Philadelphia: The Franklin Institute of the State of Pennsylvania, 1943), p. 137; that by Clinton Rossiter from *Seedtime of the Republic* (New York: Harcourt, Brace and Company, 1953), p. 304; and that by Robert E. Spiller from Margaret Denny and William H. Gilman, eds., *The American Writer and the European Tradition* (Minneapolis: University of Minnesota Press, 1950), pp. 43–44. All statements are reprinted with permission.]

CONTENTS

CONTENTS

1706	Birth in Boston.
1714	Enters Boston Grammar School.
1716–1718	Assists father in candlemaking.
1718–1723	Printer's apprentice for his brother James. Bookish inclinations. Publishes his *Dogood Papers* anonymously in the *New England Courant.*
1723–1724	Breaks indenture and runs to Philadelphia, where he works for Samuel Keimer, printer.
1724–1726	Experience in London.
1726–1736	Philadelphia. Launched upon an independent career. Founds the Junto Club 1727). Opens his own printing office (1728). Marries Deborah Read (1730). Begins *Poor Richard's Almanac* (1732).
1737	Enters politics. Appointed postmaster of Philadelphia (incumbent until 1753). Elected to the Assembly.
1742–1744	Public enterprises: invents the Franklin stove, proposes the University of Pennsylvania, establishes the American Philosophical Society, plans defense of the Province against the Indians.
1746	Begins electrical experiments.
1748	Retires from business.
1752–1754	Continues public career and scientific experiments: proves the identity of lightning and electricity, is appointed deputy Postmaster-General of the American colonies and elected a member of the British Royal Society, becomes a Commissioner at the Albany Congress to discuss Indian problems and there proposes the Albany Plan of Union.
1755	Appointed Colonel in the militia, pledging his personal property to supply Braddock's army.
1757–1762	In England to plead the cause of the Pennsylvania Assembly against the Penn Proprietaries. Secures a compromise.
1764–1775	Again in England as agent for Pennsylvania.
1764	Is examined in the House of Commons on the possible consequences in the colonies of the Stamp Act.
1770–1771	With other land speculators petitions the King for a grant of land on the Ohio River. Other colonies also appoint him their agent in England. Begins *Autobiography.*
1773–1774	Affair of the Hutchinson-Oliver letters. Dismissed as deputy Postmaster General of North America after his examination by Wedderburn before the Privy Council.
1775	Home again. Chosen a delegate to second Continental Congress.
1776	Helps frame the Declaration of Independence. The new Constitution for Pennsylvania embodies his provision for a unicameral legislature. Leaves for Paris as one of three commissioners appointed to secure aid for the American cause from the French government.
1778	Concludes treaty of defensive alliance with France.
1783	Signs treaty of peace.
1785	Returns to America. Is elected President of Pennsylvania.
1787	Delegate to the federal Constitutional Convention.
1788	Retires from public life. Completes the *Autobiography* (to the year 1757).
1790	Death.

The Clash of Issues

On Franklin's Greatness:

That he was a great genius, a great wit, a great humorist, a great satirist, and a great politician is certain. That he was a great philosopher, a great moralist, and a great statesman is more questionable.

JOHN ADAMS

[John Adams' estimate of Franklin] is by far the most searching and fairest criticism of Franklin that was ever written.

SYDNEY G. FISHER

Franklin was the earliest American whom, without limiting ourselves to national terms, we can call a very great man. When you try to define his particular greatness you run into what John Adams felt in his jealous days in Paris. Adams was a great man, but not a very great man. A great man such as Adams living with a very great man such as Franklin cannot tell the difference between himself and the other. Adams could not tell why people thought the difference to be so enormous.

CARL VAN DOREN

Urban, European, or Frontier American?

All Europe has wrought upon and metamorphosed the Yankee printer. . . . With no softening of his patriotic fibre or loss of his Yankee tang, he has acquired all the common culture and most of the master characteristics of the Age of Enlightenment. . . .

STUART P. SHERMAN

It cannot be denied that he was a benign philosopher, the most European of all the Americans of his generation, the first American "bourgeois," a practical scientist and a bold theorist. But the grandfatherly "Papa Franklin" of the rue de Passy, the astute diplomat and the clearminded patriot had worn in his youth the leather jacket of the hunter.

GILBERT CHINARD

Franklin's Moralism:

Moral America! Most moral Benjamin. Sound, satisfied Ben! . . . I do not like him.

D. H. LAWRENCE

The Puritan virtues, if we may call them that, do not add up to an especially pleasant and well-rounded personality. Franklin, however, never intended that they should stand alone, and such persons as D. H. Lawrence have done the great bourgeois no honor in confusing his full-bodied character with that of the mythical Poor Richard.

CLINTON ROSSITER

Franklin and the National Character:

In many ways this [Franklin's] is the American story. Our modern industrial research laboratories as well as our colleges and churches owe much to his identification of the moral with the natural law. The idealist in him gave him a firm basis for the acceptance of moral law; the pragmatist in him pushed him to immediate tests for his findings; and the democrat in him made him a promoter as well as a discoverer so that all mankind could be as wise as he. These, it seems to me, are the distinctive traits, not only of Franklin, but of the Americans of his day and of ours.

ROBERT E. SPILLER

All this was probably a colossal misfortune to the United States, for, despite his good fellowship and occasional good sense, Franklin represented the least praiseworthy qualities of the inhabitants of the New World: miserliness, fanatical practicality, and lack of interest in what are usually known as spiritual things. Babbittry was not a new thing in America, but he made a religion of it, and by his tremendous success with it he grafted it upon the American people so securely that the national genius is still suffering from it.

CHARLES ANGOFF

SELECTIONS FROM FRANKLIN'S AUTOBIOGRAPHY

REASONS FOR WRITING

TWYFORD, *at the Bishop of St. Asaph's,* 1771.

DEAR SON:
I have ever had a pleasure in obtaining any little anecdotes of my ancestors. You may remember the inquiries I made among the remains of my relations when you were with me in England, and the journey I undertook for that purpose. Now imagining it may be equally agreeable to you to know the circumstances of *my* life, many of which you are yet unacquainted with, and expecting a week's uninterrupted leisure in my present country retirement, I sit down to write them for you. To which I have besides some other inducements. Having emerged from the poverty and obscurity in which I was born and bred to a state of affluence and some degree of reputation in the world, and having gone so far through life with a considerable share of felicity, the conducing means I made use of, which with the blessing of God so well succeeded, my posterity may like to know, as they may find some of them suitable to their own situations, and therefore fit to be imitated.

That felicity, when I reflected on it, has induced me sometimes to say that were it offered to my choice I should have no objection to a repetition of the same life from its beginning, only asking the advantages authors have in a second edition to correct some faults of the first. So would I, if I might, besides correcting the faults, change some sinister accidents and events of it for others more favorable. But though this were denied, I should still accept the offer. However, since such a repetition is not to be expected, the next thing most like living one's life over again seems to be a *recollection* of that life, and to make that recollection as durable as possible the putting it down in writing.

Hereby, too, I shall indulge the inclination so natural in old men to be talking of themselves and their own past actions; and I shall indulge it without being troublesome to others, who, through respect to age, might think themselves obliged to give me a hearing, since this may be read or not as any one pleases. And lastly (I may as well confess it, since my denial of it will be believed by nobody), perhaps I shall a good deal gratify my own *vanity*. Indeed, I scarce ever heard or saw the introductory words, "Without vanity I may say," etc., but some vain thing immediately followed. Most people dislike vanity in others, whatever share they have of it themselves; but I give it fair quarter wherever I meet with it, being persuaded that it is often productive of good to the possessor, and to others that are within his sphere of action; and therefore, in many cases, it would not be quite absurd if a man were to thank God for his vanity among the other comforts of life.

And now I speak of thanking God, I desire with all humility to acknowledge that I owe the mentioned happiness of my past life to His kind providence, which led me to the means I used and gave them success. My belief of this induces me to *hope*, though I must not *presume*, that the same goodness will still be exercised towards me, in continuing that happiness or in enabling me to bear a fatal reverse, which I may experience as others have done, the complexion of my future fortune being known to Him only in whose power it is to bless to us even our afflictions.

YOUTH IN BOSTON

This obscure family of ours was early in the Reformation, and continued Protestants through the reign of Queen Mary, when they were sometimes in danger of trouble on account of their zeal against popery. They had got an English Bible, and to conceal and secure it, it was fastened open with tapes under and within the frame of a joint-stool. When my great-great-grandfather read it to his family, he turned up the joint-stool upon his knees, turning over the leaves then under the tapes. One of the children stood at the door to give notice if he saw the apparitor coming, who was an officer of the spiritual court. In that case the stool was turned down again upon its feet, when the Bible remained concealed under it as before. This anecdote I had from my uncle Benjamin. The family continued all of the Church of England till about the end of Charles II's reign, when some of the ministers that had been outed for nonconformity holding conventicles in Northamptonshire, Benjamin and Josiah adhered to them, and so continued all their lives: the rest of the family remained with the Episcopal church.

Josiah, my father, married young, and carried his wife with three children into New England about 1682. The conventicles having been forbidden by law and frequently disturbed induced some considerable men of his acquaintance to remove to that country, and he was prevailed with to accompany them thither, where they expected to enjoy their mode of religion with freedom. By the same wife he had four children more born there, and by a second wife ten more, in all seventeen; of which I remember thirteen sitting at one time at his table, who all grew up to be men and women, and married; I was the youngest son, and the youngest child but two, and was born in Boston, New England. My mother, the second wife, was Abiah Folger, a daughter of Peter Folger, one of the first settlers of New England, of whom honorable mention is made by Cotton Mather, in his church history of that country, entitled *Magnalia Christi Americana,* as "a godly, learned Englishman," if I remember the words rightly. I have heard that he wrote sundry small occasional pieces, but only one of them was printed, which I saw now many years since. It was written in 1675, in the homespun verse of that time and people, and addressed to those then concerned in the government there. It was in favor of liberty of conscience, and in behalf of the Baptists, Quakers, and other sectaries that had been under persecution, ascribing the Indian wars and other distresses that had befallen the country to that persecution, as so many judgments of God to punish so heinous an offense, and exhorting a repeal of those uncharitable laws. The whole appeared to me as written with a good deal of decent plainness and manly freedom. The six last concluding lines I remember, though I have forgotten the two first of the stanza; but the purport of them was that his censures proceeded from good-will and, therefore, he would be known as the author,

> Because to be a Libeller, (says he)
>   I hate it with my Heart.
> From [1]Sherburne Town where now I dwell,
>   My Name I do put here,
> Without Offense, your real Friend,
>   It is Peter Folgier.

My elder brothers were all put apprentices to different trades. I was put to the grammar school at eight years of age, my father intending to devote me, as the tithe of his sons, to the service of the church. My early readiness in learning to read (which must have been very early, as I do not remember when I could not read) and the opinion of all his friends that I should certainly make a good scholar encouraged him in this purpose of his. My uncle Benjamin, too, approved of it, and proposed to give me all his shorthand volumes of sermons, I suppose as a stock to set up with, if I would learn his character. I continued, however, at the grammar school not quite one year, though in that time I had risen gradually from the middle of the class of that year to be the head of it, and farther was removed into the next class above it, in order to go with that into the third at the end of the year. But my father, in the meantime, from a view of the expense of a college education, which having so large a family he could not well afford, and the mean living many so educated were afterwards able to obtain — reasons that he gave to his friends in my hearing — altered his first intention, took me from the grammar school, and sent me to a school for writing and arithmetic, kept by a then famous man, Mr. George Brownell, very successful in his profession generally, and that by

[1] In the Island of Nantucket.

mild, encouraging methods. Under him I acquired fair writing pretty soon, but I failed in the arithmetic, and made no progress in it. At ten years old I was taken home to assist my father in his business, which was that of a tallow-chandler and soap-boiler; a business he was not bred to, but had assumed on his arrival in New England, and on finding his dying trade would not maintain his family, being in little request. Accordingly, I was employed in cutting wick for the candles, filling the dipping mold and the molds for cast candles, attending the shop, going of errands, etc.

I disliked the trade, and had a strong inclination for the sea, but my father declared against it; however, living near the water, I was much in and about it, learned early to swim well and to manage boats; and when in a boat or canoe with other boys, I was commonly allowed to govern, especially in any case of difficulty; and upon other occasions I was generally a leader among the boys, and sometimes led them into scrapes, of which I will mention one instance, as it shows an early projecting public spirit, though not then justly conducted.

There was a salt-marsh that bounded part of the mill-pond, on the edge of which, at high water, we used to stand to fish for minnows. By much trampling, we had made it a mere quagmire. My proposal was to build a wharf there fit for us to stand upon, and I showed my comrades a large heap of stones which were intended for a new house near the marsh and which would very well suit our purpose. Accordingly, in the evening, when the workmen were gone, I assembled a number of my playfellows, and, working with them diligently like so many emmets, sometimes two or three to a stone, we brought them all away and built our little wharf. The next morning the workmen were surprised at missing the stones, which were found in our wharf. Inquiry was made after the removers; we were discovered and complained of; several of us were corrected by our fathers; and, though I pleaded the usefulness of the work, mine convinced me that nothing was useful which was not honest.

BOOKISH INCLINATIONS

From a child I was fond of reading, and all the little money that came into my hands was ever laid out in books. Pleased with the *Pilgrim's Progress*, my first collection was of John Bunyan's works in separate little volumes. I afterwards sold them to enable me to buy R. Burton's *Historical Collections;* they were small chapman's books, and cheap, forty or fifty in all. My father's little library consisted chiefly of books in polemic divinity, most of which I read and have since often regretted that at a time when I had such a thirst for knowledge, more proper books had not fallen in my way, since it was now resolved I should not be a clergyman. *Plutarch's Lives* there was, in which I read abundantly, and I still think that time spent to great advantage. There was also a book of Defoe's, called an *Essay on Projects*, and another of Dr. Mather's, called *Essays to do Good*, which perhaps gave me a turn of thinking that had an influence on some of the principal future events of my life.

This bookish inclination at length determined my father to make me a printer, though he had already one son (James) of that profession. In 1717 my brother James returned from England with a press and letters to set up his business in Boston. I liked it much better than that of my father, but still had a hankering for the sea. To prevent the apprehended effect of such an inclination, my father was impatient to have me bound to my brother. I stood out some time, but at last was persuaded, and signed the indentures when I was yet but twelve years old. I was to serve as an apprentice till I was twenty-one years of age, only I was to be allowed journeyman's wages during the last year. In a little time I made great proficiency in the business and became a useful hand to my brother. I now had access to better books. An acquaintance with the apprentices of booksellers enabled me sometimes to borrow a small one, which I was careful to return soon and clean. Often I sat up in my room reading the greatest part of the night, when the book was borrowed in the evening and to be returned early in the morning, lest it should be missed or wanted.

And after some time an ingenious tradesman, Mr. Matthew Adams, who had a pretty collection of books, and who frequented our printing-house, took notice of me, invited me to his library, and very kindly lent me such books as I chose to read. I now took a fancy to poetry, and made some little pieces; my brother, thinking it might turn to account, encouraged me, and put me on composing two occasional ballads. One was called *The Lighthouse Tragedy*, and contained an account of the drowning of Captain Worthilake with his two daughters; the other was a sailor's song, on the taking of Teach (or Blackbeard), the pirate. They were wretched stuff, in the Grub-street-ballad style; and when they were printed he sent me about the town to sell them. The first sold wonderfully, the event being recent, having made a great noise. This flattered my vanity; but my father discouraged me by ridiculing my performances and telling me verse-makers were generally beggars. So I escaped being a poet, most probably a very bad one; but as prose writing has been of great use to me in the course of my life, and was a principal means of my advancement, I shall tell you how, in such a situation, I acquired what little ability I have in that way.

There was another bookish lad in the town, John Collins by name, with whom I was intimately acquainted. We sometimes disputed; and very fond we were of argument, and very desirous of confuting one another, which disputatious turn, by the way, is apt to become a very bad habit, making people often extremely disagreeable in company by the contradiction that is necessary to bring it into practice; and thence, besides souring and spoiling the conversation, is productive of disgusts and, perhaps, enmities where you may have occasion for friendship. I had caught it by reading my father's books of dispute about religion. Persons of good sense, I have since observed, seldom fall into it, except lawyers, university men, and men of all sorts that have been bred at Edinburgh.

A question was once, somehow or other, started between Collins and me of the propriety of educating the female sex in learning, and their abilities of study. He was of opinion that it was improper, and that they were naturally unequal to it. I took the contrary side, perhaps a little for dispute's sake. He was naturally more eloquent, had a ready plenty of words, and sometimes, as I thought, bore me down more by his fluency than by the strength of his reasons. As we parted without settling the point, and were not to see one another again for some time, I sat down to put my arguments in writing, which I copied fair and sent to him. He answered, and I replied. Three or four letters of a side had passed, when my father happened to find my papers and read them. Without entering into the discussion, he took occasion to talk to me about the manner of my writing; observed that, though I had the advantage of my antagonist in correct spelling and pointing (which I owed to the printing-house), I fell far short in elegance of expression, in method, and in perspicuity, of which he convinced me by several instances. I saw the justice of his remarks, and thence grew more attentive to the *manner* in writing, and determined to endeavor at improvement.

About this time I met with an odd volume of the *Spectator*. It was the third. I had never before seen any of them. I bought it, read it over and over, and was much delighted with it. I thought the writing excellent, and wished, if possible, to imitate it. With that view I took some of the papers, and, making short hints of the sentiment in each sentence, laid them by a few days, and then, without looking at the book, tried to complete the papers again by expressing each hinted sentiment at length, and as fully as it had been expressed before, in any suitable words that should come to hand. Then I compared my *Spectator* with the original, discovered some of my faults, and corrected them. But I found I wanted a stock of words, or a readiness in recollecting and using them, which I thought I should have acquired before that time if I had gone on making verses; since the continual occasion for words of the same import, but of different length to suit the measure, or of different sound for the rhyme, would have laid me under a constant necessity of searching for variety and also have tended to fix that variety in my mind and make me master of it. Therefore, I took some of the tales and turned them into verse; and, after a time, when I had pretty well forgotten the prose, turned them back again. I also sometimes jumbled my collections of hints into confusion, and after some weeks endeavored to reduce them into the best order, before I began to form the full sentences and complete the paper. This was to teach me method in the arrangement of thoughts. By comparing my work afterwards with the original, I discovered many faults and amended them; but I sometimes had the pleasure of fancying that in certain particulars of small import I had been lucky enough to improve the method or the language, and this encouraged me to think I might possibly in time come to be a tolerable English writer, of which I was extremely ambitious. My time for these exercises and for reading was at night, after work, or before it began in the morning, or on Sundays, when I contrived to be in the printing-house alone, evading as much as I could the common attendance on public worship which my father used to exact of me when I was under his care, and which indeed I still thought a duty, though I could not, as it seemed to me, afford time to practice it.

When about sixteen years of age I happened to meet with a book, written by one Tryon, recommending a vegetable diet. I determined to go into it. My brother, being yet unmarried, did not keep house, but boarded himself and his apprentices in another family. My refusing to eat flesh occasioned an inconveniency, and I was frequently chid for my singularity. I made myself acquainted with Tryon's manner of preparing some of his dishes, such as boiling potatoes or rice, making hasty pudding, and a few others, and then proposed to my brother, that if he would give me, weekly, half the money he paid for my board, I would board myself. He instantly agreed to it, and I presently found that I could save half of what he paid me. This was an additional fund for buying books. But I had another advantage in it. My brother and the rest going from the printing-house to their meals, I remained there alone and dispatching presently my light repast, which often was no more than a biscuit or a slice of bread, a handful of raisins or a tart from the pastry-cook's, and a glass of water, had the rest of the time till their return for study, in which I made the greater progress, from that greater clearness of head and quicker apprehension which usually attend temperance in eating and drinking.

And now it was that, being on some occasion made ashamed of my ignorance in figures, which I had twice failed in learning when at school, I took Cocker's book of arithmetic, and went through the whole by myself with great ease. I also read Seller's and Sturmy's books of navigation, and became acquainted with the little geometry they contain; but never proceeded far in that science. And I read about this time Locke *On Human Understanding*, and the *Art of Thinking*, by Messrs. du Port Royal.

While I was intent on improving my language, I met with an English grammar (I think it was Greenwood's), at the end of which there were two little sketches of the arts of rhetoric and logic, the latter finishing with a specimen of a dispute in the Socratic method; and soon after I procured Xenophon's *Memorable Things of Socrates*, wherein there are many instances of the same method. I was charmed with it, adopted it, dropped my abrupt contradiction and positive argumentation, and put on the humble inquirer and doubter. And being then, from reading Shaftesbury and Collins, become a real doubter in many points of our religious doctrine, I found this method safest for myself and very embarrassing to those against whom I used it; therefore I took a delight in it, practiced it continually, and grew very artful and expert in drawing people, even of superior knowledge, into concessions, the consequences of which they did not foresee, entangling them in difficulties out of which they could not extricate themselves, and so obtaining victories that neither myself nor my cause always deserved. I continued this method some few years, but gradually left it, retaining only the habit of expressing myself in terms of modest diffidence; never using, when I advanced anything that may possibly be disputed, the words *certainly, undoubtedly,* or any others that give the air of positiveness to an opinion; but rather say, I conceive or apprehend a thing to be so or so; it appears to me, or I should think it so or so, for such and such reasons; or I imagine it to be so; or it is so, if I am not mistaken. This habit, I believe, has been of great advantage to me when I have had occasion to inculcate my opinions and persuade men into measures that I have been from time to time engaged in pro-

moting; and, as the chief ends of conversation are to *inform* or to be *informed*, to *please* or to *persuade*, I wish well-meaning, sensible men would not lessen their power of doing good by a positive, assuming manner that seldom fails to disgust, tends to create opposition and to defeat every one of those purposes for which speech was given to us, to wit, giving or receiving information or pleasure. For if you would *inform*, a positive dogmatical manner in advancing your sentiments may provoke contradiction and prevent a candid attention. If you wish information and improvement from the knowledge of others, and yet at the same time express yourself as firmly fixed in your present opinions, modest, sensible men, who do not love disputation, will probably leave you undisturbed in the possession of your error. And by such a manner, you can seldom hope to recommend yourself in *pleasing* your hearers, or to persuade those whose concurrence you desire.

THE NEW ENGLAND COURANT

My brother had, in 1720 or 21, begun to print a newspaper. It was the second that appeared in America, and was called the *New England Courant*. The only one before it was the *Boston News-Letter*. I remember his being dissuaded by some of his friends from the undertaking, as not likely to succeed, one newspaper being, in their judgment, enough for America. At this time (1771) there are not less than five-and-twenty. He went on, however, with the undertaking, and after having worked in composing the types and printing off the sheets, I was employed to carry the papers through the streets to the customers.

He had some ingenious men among his friends, who amused themselves by writ-

ing little pieces for this paper, which gained it credit and made it more in demand, and these gentlemen often visited us. Hearing their conversations, and their accounts of the approbation their papers were received with, I was excited to try my hand among them; but, being still a boy, and suspecting that my brother would object to printing anything of mine in his paper if he knew it to be mine, I contrived to disguise my hand and, writing an anonymous paper, I put it in at night under the door of the printing-house. It was found in the morning and communicated to his writing friends when they called in as usual. They read it, commented on it in my hearing, and I had the exquisite pleasure of finding it met with their approbation, and that, in their different guesses at the author, none were named but men of some character among us for learning and ingenuity. I suppose now that I was rather lucky in my judges, and that perhaps they were not really so very good ones as I then esteemed them.

Encouraged, however, by this, I wrote and conveyed in the same way to the press several more papers which were equally approved; and I kept my secret till my small fund of sense for such performances was pretty well exhausted, and then I discovered it, when I began to be considered a little more by my brother's acquaintance, and in a manner that did not quite please him, as he thought, probably with reason, that it tended to make me too vain. And perhaps this might be one occasion of the differences that we began to have about this time. Though a brother, he considered himself as my master, and me as his apprentice, and accordingly expected the same services from me as he would from another, while I thought he demeaned me too much in some he required of me, who from a brother expected more indulgence. Our disputes were often brought before our father, and I fancy I was either generally in the right, or else a better pleader, because the judgment was generally in my favor. But my brother was passionate, and had often beaten me, which I took extremely amiss; and, thinking my apprenticeship very tedious, I was continually wishing for some opportunity of shortening it, which at length offered in a manner unexpected.[2]

One of the pieces in our newspaper on some political point, which I have now forgotten, gave offense to the Assembly.

He was taken up, censured, and imprisoned for a month, by the speaker's warrant, I suppose because he would not discover his author. I too was taken up and examined before the council; but, though I did not give them any satisfaction, they contented themselves with admonishing me, and dismissed me, considering me, perhaps, as an apprentice who was bound to keep his master's secrets.

During my brother's confinement, which I resented a good deal, notwithstanding our private differences, I had the management of the paper; and I made bold to give our rulers some rubs in it, which my brother took very kindly, while others began to consider me in an unfavorable light, as a young genius that had a turn for libeling and satire. My brother's discharge was accompanied with an order of the House (a very odd one), that "James Franklin should no longer print the paper called the *New England Courant.*"

There was a consultation held in our printing-house among his friends what he should do in this case. Some proposed to evade the order by changing the name of the paper; but my brother seeing inconveniences in that, it was finally concluded on as a better way to let it be printed for the future under the name of *Benjamin Franklin;* and to avoid the censure of the Assembly, that might fall on him as still printing it by his apprentice, the contrivance was that my old indenture should be returned to me, with a full discharge on the back of it, to be shown on occasion; but to secure to him the benefit of my service, I was to sign new indentures for the remainder of the term, which were to be kept private. A very flimsy scheme it was; however, it was immediately executed, and the paper went on accordingly under my name for several months.

At length, a fresh difference arising be-

---

[2] I fancy his harsh and tyrannical treatment of me might be a means of impressing me with that aversion to arbitrary power that has stuck to me through my whole life.

tween my brother and me, I took upon me to assert my freedom, presuming that he would not venture to produce the new indentures. It was not fair in me to take this advantage, and this I therefore reckon one of the first errata of my life; but the unfairness of it weighed little with me when under the impressions of resentment for the blows his passion too often urged him to bestow upon me, though he was otherwise not an ill-natured man; perhaps I was too saucy and provoking.

When he found I would leave him, he took care to prevent my getting employment in any other printing-house of the town, by going round and speaking to every master, who accordingly refused to give me work. I then thought of going to New York, as the nearest place where there was a printer; and I was the rather inclined to leave Boston when I reflected that I has already made myself a little obnoxious to the governing party, and, from the arbitrary proceedings of the Assembly in my brother's case, it was likely I might, if I stayed, soon bring myself into scrapes; and farther, that my indiscreet disputations about religion began to make me pointed at with horror by good people as an infidel or atheist. I determined on the point, but my father now siding with my brother, I was sensible that, if I attempted to go openly, means would be used to prevent me. My friend Collins, therefore, undertook to

manage a little for me. He agreed with the captain of a New York sloop for my passage, under the notion of my being a young acquaintance of his, that had got a naughty girl with child, whose friends would compel me to marry her, and therefore I could not appear or come away publicly. So I sold some of my books to raise a little money, was taken on board privately, and as we had a fair wind, in three days I found myself in New York, near three hundred miles from home, a boy of but seventeen, without the least recommendation to, or knowledge of, any person in the place, and with very little money in my pocket.

My inclinations for the sea were by this time worn out, or I might now have gratified them. But, having a trade, and supposing myself a pretty good workman, I offered my service to the printer in the place, old Mr. William Bradford, who had been the first printer in Pennsylvania, but removed from thence upon the quarrel of George Keith. He could give me no employment, having little to do and help enough already; but, says he, "My son at Philadelphia has lately lost his principal hand, Aquila Rose, by death; if you go thither, I believe he may employ you." Philadelphia was one hundred miles further; I set out, however, in a boat for Amboy, leaving my chest and things to follow me round by sea.

ARRIVAL IN PHILADELPHIA

I have been the more particular in this description of my journey, and shall be so of my first entry into that city, that you may in your mind compare such unlikely beginnings with the figure I have since made there. I was in my working dress, my best clothes being to come round by sea. I was dirty from my journey; my

pockets were stuffed out with shirts and stockings; I knew no soul nor where to look for lodging. I was fatigued with traveling, rowing, and want of rest; I was very hungry; and my whole stock of cash consisted of a Dutch dollar and about a shilling in copper. The latter I gave the people of the boat for my passage, who at first refused it, on account of my rowing; but I insisted on their taking it, a man being sometimes more generous when he has but a little money than when he has plenty, perhaps through fear of being thought to have but little.

Then I walked up the street, gazing about, till near the market-house I met a boy with bread. I had made many a meal on bread, and, inquiring where he got it, I went immediately to the baker's he directed me to, in Second Street, and asked for biscuit, intending such as we had in Boston; but they, it seems, were not made in Philadelphia. Then I asked for a three-penny loaf, and was told they had none such. So, not considering or knowing the difference of money, and the greater cheapness nor the names of his bread, I bade him give me three-penny-worth of any sort. He gave me, accordingly, three great puffy rolls. I was surprised at the quantity, but took it, and, having no room in my pockets, walked off with a roll under each arm, and eating the other. Thus I went up Market Street as far as Fourth Street, passing by the door of Mr. Read, my future wife's father; when she, standing at the door, saw me, and thought I made, as I certainy did, a most awkward, ridiculous appearance. Then I turned and went down Chestnut Street and part of Walnut Street, eating my roll all the way, and, coming round, found myself again at Market Street wharf, near the boat I came in, to which I went for a draught of the river water; and, being filled with one of my rolls, gave the other two to a woman and her child that came down the river in the boat with us, and were waiting to go farther. . . .

DEISTIC PRINCIPLES

Before I enter upon my public appearance in business, it may be well to let you know the then state of my mind with regard to my principles and morals, that you may see how far those influenced the future events of my life. My parents had early given me religious impressions, and brought me through my childhood piously in the dissenting way. But I was scarce fifteen, when, after doubting by turns of several points, as I found them disputed in the different books I read, I began to doubt of Revelation itself. Some books against deism fell into my hands; they were said to be the substance of sermons preached at Boyle's lectures. It happened that they wrought an effect on me quite contrary to what was intended by them; for the arguments of the deists, which were quoted to be refuted, appeared to me much stronger than the refutations; in short, I soon became a thorough deist.

My arguments perverted some others, particularly Collins and Ralph; but each of them having afterwards wronged me greatly without the least compunction, and recollecting Keith's conduct towards me (who was another free-thinker), and my own towards Vernon and Miss Read, which at times gave me great trouble, I began to suspect that this doctrine, though it might be true, was not very useful. My London pamphlet, which had for its motto these lines of Dryden:

Whatever is, is right. Though purblind Man
Sees but a Part of the Chain, the nearest Link,
His Eyes not carrying to the equal Beam,
That poises all, above.

and from the attributes of God, his infinite wisdom, goodness, and power, concluded that nothing could possibly be wrong in the world, and that vice and virtue were empty distinctions, no such things existing, appeared now not so clever a performance as I once thought it; and I doubted whether some error had not insinuated itself unperceived into my argument, so as to infect all that followed, as is common in metaphysical reasonings.

I grew convinced that *truth, sincerity* and *integrity* in dealings between man and man were of the utmost importance to the felicity of life; and I formed written resolutions (which still remain in my journal book), to practice them ever while I lived. Revelation had indeed no weight with me as such; but I entertained an opinion that, though certain actions might not be bad *because* they were forbidden by it, or good *because* it commanded them, yet probably these actions might be forbidden *because* they were bad for us, or commanded *because* they were beneficial to us in their own natures, all the circumstances of things considered. And this persuasion, with the kind hand of Providence or some guardian angel, or accidental favorable circumstances and situations, or all together, preserved me through this dangerous time of youth, and the hazardous situations I was sometimes in among strangers, remote from the eye and advice of my father, without any *willful* gross immorality or injustice, that might have been expected from my want of religion. I say *willful,* because the instances I have mentioned had something of *necessity* in them, from my youth, inexperience, and the knavery of others. I had therefore a tolerable character to begin the world with; I valued it properly, and determined to preserve it.

ESTABLISHMENT IN BUSINESS AND MARRIAGE

I now opened a little stationer's shop. I had in it blanks of all sorts, the correctest that ever appeared among us, being assisted in that by my friend Breintnal. I had also paper, parchment, chapmen's books, etc. One Whitemash, a compositor I had known in London, an excellent workman, now came to me, and worked with me constantly and diligently; and I took an apprentice, the son of Aquila Rose.

I began now gradually to pay off the debt I was under for the printing-house. In order to secure my credit and character as a tradesman, I took care not only to be in *reality* industrious and frugal, but to avoid all *appearances* of the contrary. I dressed plainly; I was seen at no places of idle diversion. I never went out afishing or shooting; a book, indeed, sometimes debauched me from my work, but that was seldom, snug, and gave no scandal; and, to show that I was not above my business, I sometimes brought home the paper I purchased at the stores through the streets on a wheelbarrow. Thus being esteemed an industrious, thriving young man, and paying duly for what I bought, the merchants who imported stationery solicited my custom; others proposed supplying me with books; I went on swimmingly. In the meantime, Keimer's credit and business declining daily, he was at last forced to sell his printing-house to satisfy his creditors. He went to Barbados, and there lived some years in very poor circumstances.

His apprentice, David Harry, whom I had instructed while I worked with him, set up in his place at Philadelphia, having bought his materials. I was at first apprehensive of a powerful rival in Harry, as his friends were very able, and had a good deal of interest. I therefore proposed a partnership to him, which he, fortunately for me, rejected with scorn. He was very proud, dressed like a gentleman, lived expensively, took much diversion and pleasure abroad, ran in debt, and neglected his business; upon which, all business left him; and, finding nothing to do, he followed Keimer to Barbados, taking the printing-house with him. There this apprentice employed his former master as a journeyman; they quarreled often; Harry went continually behindhand, and at length was forced to sell his types and return to his country work in Pennsylvania. The person that bought them employed Keimer to use them, but in a few years he died.

There remained now no competitor with me at Philadelphia but the old one, Bradford, who was rich and easy, did a little printing now and then by straggling hands, but was not very anxious about it. However, as he kept the post-office, it was imagined he had better opportunities of obtaining news; his paper was thought a better distributer of advertisements than mine, and therefore had many more, which was a profitable thing to him, and a disadvantage to me; for, though I did indeed receive and send papers by the post, yet the public opinion was otherwise, for what I did send was by bribing the riders, who took them privately, Bradford being unkind enough to forbid it, which occasioned some resentment on my part; and I thought so meanly of him for it, that when I afterward came into his situation I took care never to imitate it.

I had hitherto continued to board with Godfrey, who lived in part of my house with his wife and children, and had one side of the shop for his glazier's business, though he worked little, being always absorbed in his mathematics. Mrs. Godfrey projected a match for me with a relation's daughter, took opportunities of bringing us often together, till a serious courtship

on my part ensued, the girl being in herself very deserving. The old folks encouraged me by continual invitations to supper, and by leaving us together, till at length it was time to explain. Mrs. Godfrey managed our little treaty. I let her know that I expected as much money with their daughter as would pay off my remaining debt for the printing-house, which I believe was not then above a hundred pounds. She brought me word they had no such sum to spare; I said they might mortgage their house in the loan-office. The answer to this after some days was that they did not approve the match; that, on inquiry of Bradford, they had been informed the printing business was not a profitable one, the types would soon be worn out, and more wanted, that S. Keimer and D. Harry had failed one after the other, and I should probably soon follow them; and therefore I was forbidden the house, and the daughter shut up.

Whether this was a real change of sentiment or only artifice, on a supposition of our being too far engaged in affection to retract, and therefore that we should steal a marriage, which would leave them at liberty to give or withhold what they pleased, I know not; but I suspected the latter, resented it, and went no more. Mrs. Godfrey brought me afterwards some more favorable accounts of their disposition, and would have drawn me on again; but I declared absolutely my resolution to have nothing more to do with that family. This was resented by the Godfreys; we differed, and they removed, leaving me the whole house, and I resolved to take no more inmates.

But this affair having turned my thoughts to marriage, I looked around me and made overtures of acquaintance in other places; but soon found that, the business of a printer being generally thought a poor one, I was not to expect money with a wife, unless with such a one as I should not otherwise think agreeable. In the meantime that hard-to-be-governed passion of youth hurried me frequently into intrigues with low women that fell in my way, which were attended with some expense and great inconvenience, besides a continual risk to my health by a distemper, which of all things I dreaded, though by great good luck I escaped it.

A friendly correspondence as neighbors and old acquaintances had continued between me and Mrs. Read's family, who all had a regard for me from the time of my first lodging in their house. I was often invited there and consulted in their affairs, wherein I sometimes was of service. I pitied poor Miss Read's unfortunate situation, who was generally dejected, seldom cheerful, and avoided company. I considered my giddiness and inconstancy when in London as in a great degree the cause of her unhappiness, though the mother was good enough to think the fault more her own than mine, as she had prevented our marrying before I went thither, and persuaded the other match in my absence. Our mutual affection was revived, but there were now great objections to our union. That match was indeed looked upon as invalid, a preceding wife being said to be living in England; but this could not easily be proved, because of the distance; and though there was a report of his death, it was not certain. Then, though it should be true, he had left many debts, which his successor might be called upon to pay. We ventured, however, over all these difficulties, and I took her to wife, September 1st, 1730. None of the inconveniences happened that we had apprehended; she proved a good and faithful helpmate, assisted me much by attending the shop; we throve together, and have ever mutually endeavored to make each other happy. Thus I corrected that great erratum as well as I could. . . .

PROJECT FOR ARRIVING AT MORAL PERFECTION

It was about this time I conceived the bold and arduous project of arriving at moral perfection. I wished to live without committing any fault at any time; I would conquer all that either natural inclination, custom, or company might lead me into. As I knew, or thought I knew, what was right and wrong, I did not see why I might not always do the one and avoid the other. But I soon found I had undertaken a task of more difficulty than I had imagined. While my care was employed in guarding against one fault, I was often surprised by another; habit took the advantage of inattention; inclination was sometimes too strong for reason. I concluded, at length, that the mere speculative conviction that it was our interest to be completely virtuous was not sufficient to prevent our slipping; and that the contrary habits must be broken, and good ones acquired and established, before we can have any dependence on a steady, uniform rectitude of conduct. For this purpose I therefore contrived the following method.

In the various enumerations of the moral virtues I had met with in my reading, I found the catalogue more or less numerous, as different writers included more or fewer ideas under the same name. Temperance, for example, was by some confined to eating and drinking, while by others it was extended to mean the moderating every other pleasure, appetite, inclination, or passion, bodily or mental, even to our avarice and ambition. I proposed to myself, for the sake of clearness, to use rather more names, with fewer ideas annexed to each, than a few names with more ideas; and I included under thirteen names of virtues all that at that time occurred to me as necessary or desirable, and annexed to each a short precept, which fully expressed the extent I gave to its meaning.

These names of virtues, with their precepts, were:

1. TEMPERANCE.
Eat not to dullness; drink not to elevation.

2. SILENCE.
Speak not but what may benefit others or yourself; avoid trifling conversation.

3. ORDER.
Let all your things have their places; let each part of your business have its time.

4. RESOLUTION.
Resolve to perform what you ought; perform without fail what you resolve.

5. FRUGALITY.
Make no expense but to do good to others or yourself; i.e., waste nothing.

6. INDUSTRY.
Lose no time; be always employed in something useful; cut off all unnecessary actions.

7. SINCERITY.
Use no hurtful deceit; think innocently and justly, and, if you speak, speak accordingly.

8. JUSTICE.
Wrong none by doing injuries, or omitting the benefits that are your duty.

9. MODERATION.
Avoid extremes; forbear resenting injuries so much as you think they deserve.

10. CLEANLINESS.
Tolerate no uncleanliness in body, clothes, or habitation.

11. TRANQUILLITY.
Be not disturbed at trifles, or at accidents common or unavoidable.

12. CHASTITY
Rarely use venery but for health or offspring, never to dullness, weakness, or the injury of your own or another's peace or reputation.

13. HUMILITY.
Imitate Jesus and Socrates.

My intention being to acquire the *habitude* of all these virtues, I judged it would be well not to distract my attention by attempting the whole at once, but to fix it on one of them at a time; and, when I should be master of that, then to proceed to another, and so on, till I should have gone through the thirteen; and, as the previous acquisition of some might facilitate the acquisition of certain others, I arranged them with that view, as they stand above. *Temperance* first, as it tends to procure that coolness and clearness of head, which is so necessary where constant vigilance was to be kept up, and guard maintained against the unremitting attraction of ancient habits, and the force of perpetual temptations. This being acquired and established, *Silence* would be more easy; and my desire being to gain knowledge at the same time that I improved in virtue, and considering that in conversation it was obtained rather by the use of the ears than of the tongue, and therefore wishing to break a habit I was getting into of prattling, punning, and joking, which only made me acceptable to trifling company, I gave *Silence* the second place. This and the next, *Order,* I expected would allow me more time for attending to my project and my studies. *Resolution,* once become habitual, would keep me firm in my endeavors to obtain all the subsequent virtues; *Frugality* and *Industry* freeing me from my remaining debt, and producing affluence and independence, would make more easy the practice of *Sincerity* and *Justice,* etc., etc. Conceiving then, that, agreeably to the advice of Pythagoras in his Golden Verses, daily examination would be necessary, I contrived the following method for conducting that examination.

I made a little book, in which I allotted a page for each of the virtues. I ruled each page with red ink, so as to have seven columns, one for each day of the week, marking each column with a letter for the day. I crossed these columns with thirteen red lines, marking the beginning of each line with the first letter of one of the virtues, on which line, and in its proper column, I might mark, by a little black spot, every fault I found upon examination to have been committed respecting that virtue upon that day.

I determined to give a week's strict attention to each of the virtues successively. Thus, in the first week, my great guard was to avoid every the least offence against *Temperance,* leaving the other virtues to their ordinary chance, only marking every evening the faults of the day. Thus, if in the first week I could keep my first line, marked T, clear of spots, I supposed the habit of that virtue so much strengthened, and its opposite weakened, that I might venture extending my attention to include the next, and for the following week keep both lines clear of spots. Proceeding thus to the last, I could go through a course complete in thirteen weeks, and four courses in a year. And like him who, having a garden to weed, does not attempt to eradicate all the bad

herbs at once, which would exceed his reach and his strength, but works on one of the beds at a time, and, having accomplished the first, proceeds to a second, so I should have, I hoped, the encouraging pleasure of seeing on my pages the progress I made in virtue, by clearing successively my lines of their spots, till in the end, by a number of courses, I should be happy in viewing a clean book, after a thirteen weeks' daily examination.

Form of the pages.

TEMPERANCE.						
EAT NOT TO DULLNESS; DRINK NOT TO ELEVATION.						
	S.	M.	T.	W.	T.	F.	S.
T.							
S.	❋	❋		❋		❋	
O.	❋ ❋	❋	❋			❋	❋	❋
R.				❋		❋	
F.		❋				❋	
I.			❋				
S.							
J.							
M.							
C.							
T.							
C.							
H.							

This my little book had for its motto these lines from Addison's *Cato:*

Here will I hold. If there's a power above us
(And that there is, all nature cries aloud
Thro' all her works), He must delight in
   virtue;
And that which he delights in must be happy.

Another from Cicero,

O vitæ Philosophia dux! O virtutum inda-
gatrix expultrixque vitiorum! Unus dies, bene
et ex præceptis tuis actus, peccanti immorta-
litati est anteponendus.

Another from the Proverbs of Solomon,
speaking of wisdom or virtue:

Length of days is in her right hand, and in
her left hand riches and honour. Her ways
are ways of pleasantness, and all her paths
are peace. iii. 16, 17.

And conceiving God to be the fountain
of wisdom, I thought it right and necessary to solicit his assistance for obtaining
it; to this end I formed the following little
prayer, which was prefixed to my tables
of examination, for daily use.

O powerful Goodness! bountiful Father!
merciful Guide! Increase in me that wisdom
which discovers my truest interest. Strengthen
my resolutions to perform what that wisdom
dictates. Accept my kind offices to thy other
children as the only return in my power for
thy continual favours to me.

I used also sometimes a little prayer
which I took from Thomson's Poems, viz.:

Father of light and life, thou Good Supreme!
O teach me what is good; teach me Thyself!
Save me from folly, vanity, and vice,
From every low pursuit; and fill my soul
With knowledge, conscious peace, and virtue
  pure;
Sacred, substantial, never-fading bliss!

The precept of *Order* requiring that
*every part of my business should have its
allotted time,* one page in my little book
contained the following scheme of employment for the twenty-four hours of a
natural day.

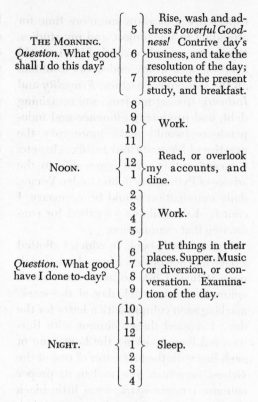

THE MORNING. *Question.* What good shall I do this day?	5 6 7	Rise, wash and ad-dress *Powerful Good-ness!* Contrive day's business, and take the resolution of the day; prosecute the present study, and breakfast.
	8 9 10 11	Work.
NOON.	12 1	Read, or overlook my accounts, and dine.
	2 3 4 5	Work.
Question. What good have I done to-day?	6 7 8 9	Put things in their places. Supper. Music or diversion, or con-versation. Examina-tion of the day.
NIGHT.	10 11 12 1 2 3 4	Sleep.

I entered upon the execution of this
plan for self-examination, and continued
it with occasional intermissions for some
time. I was surprised to find myself so
much fuller of faults than I had imagined; but I had the satisfaction of seeing
them diminish. To avoid the trouble of
renewing now and then my little book,
which, by scraping out the marks on the
paper of old faults to make room for new
ones in a new course, became full of holes,
I transferred my tables and precepts to
the ivory leaves of a memorandum book,
on which the lines were drawn with red
ink, that made a durable stain, and on
those lines I marked my faults with a
black-lead pencil, which marks I could
easily wipe out with a wet sponge. After
a while I went through one course only in
a year, and afterward only one in several
years, till at length I omitted them en-

tirely, being employed in voyages and business abroad, with a multiplicity of affairs that interfered; but I always carried my little book with me.

My scheme of ORDER gave me the most trouble; and I found that, though it might be practicable where a man's business was such as to leave him the disposition of his time, that of a journeyman printer, for instance, it was not possible to be exactly observed by a master, who must mix with the world, and often receive people of business at their own hours. *Order*, too, with regard to places for things, papers, etc., I found extremely difficult to acquire. I had not been early accustomed to it, and, having an exceeding good memory, I was not so sensible of the inconvenience attending want of method. This article, therefore, cost me so much painful attention, and my faults in it vexed me so much, and I made so little progress in amendment, and had such frequent relapses, that I was almost ready to give up the attempt and content myself with a faulty character in that respect, like the man who, in buying an ax of a smith, my neighbor, desired to have the whole of its surface as bright as the edge. The smith consented to grind it bright for him if he would turn the wheel; he turned, while the smith pressed the broad face of the ax hard and heavily on the stone, which made the turning of it very fatiguing. The man came every now and then from the wheel to see how the work went on, and at length would take his ax as it was, without farther grinding. "No," said the smith, "turn on, turn on; we shall have it bright by-and-by; as yet, it is only speckled." "Yes," says the man, "but I think I like a speckled ax best." And I believe this may have been the case with many, who having for want of some such means as I employed found the difficulty of obtaining good and breaking bad

habits in other points of vice and virtue, have given up the struggle, and concluded that *"a speckled ax was best";* for something that pretended to be reason, was every now and then suggesting to me that such extreme nicety as I exacted of myself might be a kind of foppery in morals, which, if it were known, would make me ridiculous; that a perfect character might be attended with the inconvenience of being envied and hated; and that a benevolent man should allow a few faults in himself, to keep his friends in countenance.

In truth, I found myself incorrigible with respect to Order; and now I am grown old, and my memory bad, I feel very sensibly the want of it. But on the whole, though I never arrived at the perfection I had been so ambitious of obtaining, but fell far short of it, yet I was, by the endeavor, a better and a happier man than I otherwise should have been if I had not attempted it; as those who aim at perfect writing by imitating the engraved copies, though they never reach the wished-for excellence of those copies, their hand is mended by the endeavor, and is tolerable while it continues fair and legible.

It may be well my posterity should be informed that to this little artifice, with the blessing of God, their ancestor owed the constant felicity of his life, down to his 79th year, in which this is written. What reverses may attend the remainder is in the hand of Providence; but if they arrive the reflection on past happiness enjoyed ought to help his bearing them with more resignation. To Temperance he ascribes his long-continued health and what is still left to him of a good constitution; to Industry and Frugality, the early easiness of his circumstances and acquisition of his fortune, with all that knowledge that enabled him to be a useful citizen, and obtained for him some degree of reputation among the learned; to Sincerity and Justice, the confidence of his country, and the honorable employs it conferred upon him; and to the joint influence of the whole mass of the virtues, even in the imperfect state he was able to acquire them, all that evenness of temper, and that cheerfulness in conversation, which makes his company still sought for, and agreeable even to his younger acquaintance. I hope, therefore, that some of my descendants may follow the example and reap the benefit.

It will be remarked that, though my scheme was not wholly without religion, there was in it no mark of any of the distinguishing tenets of any particular sect. I had purposely avoided them; for, being fully persuaded of the utility and excellency of my method, and that it might be serviceable to people in all religions, and intending some time or other to publish it, I would not have anything in it that should prejudice anyone, of any sect, against it. I purposed writing a little comment on each virtue, in which I would have shown the advantages of possessing it, and the mischiefs attending its opposite vice; and I should have called my book "The Art of Virtue,"[3] because it would have shown the means and manner of obtaining virtue, which would have distinguished it from the mere exhortation to be good, that does not instruct and indicate the means, but is like the apostle's man of verbal charity, who only without showing to the naked and hungry how or where they might get clothes or victuals, exhorted them to be fed and clothed. — James ii. 15, 16.

But it so happened that my intention of writing and publishing this comment

was never fulfilled. I did, indeed, from time to time, put down short hints of the sentiments, reasonings, etc., to be made use of in it, some of which I have still by me; but the necessary close attention to private business in the earlier part of my life, and public business since, have occasioned my postponing it; for, it being connected in my mind with *a great and extensive project,* that required the whole man to execute, and which an unforeseen succession of employs prevented my attending to, it has hitherto remained unfinished.

In this piece it was my design to explain and enforce this doctrine, that vicious actions are not hurtful because they are forbidden, but forbidden because they are hurtful, the nature of man alone considered; that it was, therefore, every one's interest to be virtuous who wished to be happy even in this world; and I should, from this circumstance (there being always in the world a number of rich merchants, nobility, states, and princes, who have need of honest instruments for the management of their affairs, and such being so rare), have endeavored to convince young persons that no qualities were so likely to make a poor man's fortune as those of probity and integrity.

My list of virtues contained at first but twelve; but a Quaker friend having kindly informed me that I was generally thought proud; that my pride showed itself frequently in conversation; that I was not content with being in the right when discussing any point, but was overbearing, and rather insolent, of which he convinced me by mentioning several instances; I determined endeavoring to cure myself if I could, of this vice or folly among the rest, and I added *Humility* to my list, giving an extensive meaning to the word.

I cannot boast of much success in ac-

---

[3] Nothing so likely to make a man's fortune as virtue. [FRANKLIN'S NOTE.]

quiring the *reality* of this virtue, but I had a good deal with regard to the *appearance* of it. I made it a rule to forbear all direct contradiction to the sentiments of others, and all positive assertion of my own. I even forbid myself, agreeably to the old laws of our Junto, the use of every word or expression in the language that imported a fixed opinion, such as *certainly, undoubtedly,* etc., and I adopted, instead of them, *I conceive, I apprehend,* or *I imagine* a thing to be so or so; or it *so appears to me at present.* When another asserted something that I thought an error, I denied myself the pleasure of contradicting him abruptly, and of showing immediately some absurdity in his proposition; and in answering I began by observing that in certain cases or circumstances his opinion would be right, but in the present case there *appeared* or *seemed* to me some difference, etc. I soon found the advantage of this change in my manner; the conversations I engaged in went on more pleasantly. The modest way in which I proposed my opinions procured them a readier reception and less contradiction; I had less mortification when I was found to be in the wrong, and I more easily prevailed with others to give up their mistakes and join with me when I happened to be in the right.

And this mode, which I at first put on with some violence to natural inclination, became at length so easy, and so habitual to me, that perhaps for these fifty years past no one has ever heard a dogmatical expression escape me. And to this habit (after my character of integrity) I think it principally owing that I had early so much weight with my fellow-citizens when I proposed new institutions, or alterations in the old, and so much influence in public councils when I became a member; for I was but a bad speaker, never eloquent, subject to much hesitation in my choice of words, hardly correct in language, and yet I generally carried my points.

In reality, there is, perhaps, no one of our natural passions so hard to subdue as *pride.* Disguise it, struggle with it, beat it down, stifle it, mortify it as much as one pleases, it is still alive, and will every now and then peep out and show itself; you will see it, perhaps, often in this history; for, even if I could conceive that I had completely overcome it, I should probably be proud of my humility.

Thus far written at Passy, 1784. . . .

ELECTRICAL EXPERIMENTS

In 1746, being at Boston, I met there with a Dr. Spence, who was lately arrived from Scotland and showed me some electric experiments. They were imperfectly performed, as he was not very expert; but, being on a subject quite new to me, they equally surprised and pleased me. Soon after my return to Philadelphia, our library company received from Mr. P. Collinson, Fellow of the Royal Society of London, a present of a glass tube, with some account of the use of it in making such experiments. I eagerly seized the opportunity of repeating what I had seen at Boston; and by much practice, acquired great readiness in performing those, also, which we had an account of from England, adding a number of new ones. I say much practice, for my house was continually full for some time with people who came to see these new wonders.

To divide a little this incumbrance among my friends, I caused a number of similar tubes to be blown at our glass-house, with which they furnished themselves, so that we had at length several performers. Among these, the principal was Mr. Kinnersley, an ingenious neighbor, who, being out of business, I encouraged to undertake showing the experiments for money, and drew up for him two lectures, in which the experiments were ranged in such order, and accompanied with such explanations in such method, as that the foregoing should assist in comprehending the following. He procured an elegant apparatus for the purpose, in which all the little machines that I had roughly made for myself were nicely formed by instrument-makers. His lectures were well attended, and gave great satisfaction; and after some time he went through the colonies, exhibiting them in every capital town, and picked up some money. In the West India islands, indeed, it was with difficulty the experiments could be made, from the general moisture of the air.

Obliged as we were to Mr. Collinson for his present of the tube, etc., I thought it right he should be informed of our success in using it, and wrote him several letters containing accounts of our experiments. He got them read in the Royal Society, where they were not at first thought worth so much notice as to be printed in their *Transactions*. One paper, which I wrote for Mr. Kinnersley on the sameness of lightning with electricity, I sent to Dr. Mitchel, an acquaintance of mine, and one of the members also of that society, who wrote me word that it had been read, but was laughed at by the connoisseurs. The papers, however, being shown to Dr. Fothergill, he thought them of too much value to be stifled, and advised the printing of them. Mr. Collinson then gave them to Cave for publication in his *Gentleman's Magazine;* but he chose to print them separately in a pamphlet, and Dr. Fothergill wrote the preface. Cave, it seems, judged rightly for his profit, for by the additions that arrived afterward they swelled to a quarto volume, which has had five editions, and cost him nothing for copy-money.

It was, however, some time before those papers were much taken notice of in England. A copy of them happening to fall into the hands of the Count de Buffon, a philosopher deservedly of great reputation in France, and, indeed, all over Europe, he prevailed with M. Dalibard to translate them into French, and they were printed at Paris. The publication offended the Abbé Nollet, preceptor in natural philosophy to the royal family, and an able experimenter, who had formed and published a theory of electricity, which then had the general vogue. He could not at first believe that such a work came from America, and said it must have been fabricated by his enemies at Paris to decry his system. Afterwards, having been assured that there really existed such a person as Franklin at Philadelphia, which he had doubted, he wrote and published a volume of letters, chiefly addressed to me, defending his theory, and denying the verity of my experiments, and of the positions deduced from them.

I once purposed answering the Abbé, and actually began the answer; but, on consideration that my writings contained a description of experiments which any one might repeat and verify, and if not to be verified, could not be defended; or of observations offered as conjectures, and not delivered dogmatically, therefore not laying me under any obligation to defend them; and reflecting that a dispute between two persons, writing in different languages, might be lengthened greatly by mistranslations, and thence misconceptions of one another's meaning, much of one of the Abbé's letters being founded on error in the translation, I concluded to let my papers shift for themselves, believing it was better to spend what time I could spare from public business in making new experiments than in disputing about those already made. I therefore never answed M. Nollet, and the event gave me no cause to repent my silence; for my friend M. le Roy, of the Royal Academy of Sciences, took up my cause and refuted him; my book was translated into the Italian, German, and Latin languages; and the doctrine it contained was by degrees universally adopted by the philosophers of Europe, in preference to that of the Abbé; so that he lived to see himself the last of his sect, except Monsieur B——, of Paris, his *élève* and immediate disciple.

What gave my book the more sudden and general celebrity was the success of one of its proposed experiments, made by Messrs. Dalibard and De Lor at Marly, for drawing lightning from the clouds. This engaged the public attention everywhere. M. de Lor, who had an apparatus for experimental philosophy, and lectured in that branch of science, undertook to repeat what he called the Philadelphia Experiments, and after they were performed before the king and court, all the curious of Paris flocked to see them. I will not swell this narrative with an account of that capital experiment, nor of the infinite pleasure I received in the success of a similar one I made soon after with a kite at Philadelphia, as both are to be found in the histories of electricity.

Dr. Wright, an English physician, when at Paris wrote to a friend who was of the Royal Society an account of the high esteem my experiments were in among the learned abroad, and of their wonder that my writings had been so little noticed in England. The society, on this, resumed the consideration of the letters that had been read to them; and the celebrated Dr. Watson drew up a summary account of them, and of all I had afterwards sent to England on the subject, which he accompanied with some praise of the writer. This summary was then printed in their *Transactions;* and some members of the society in London, particularly the very ingenious Mr. Canton, having verified the experiment of procuring lightning from the clouds by a pointed rod, and acquainting them with the success, they soon made me more than amends for the slight with which they had before treated me. Without my having made any application for that honor, they chose me a member, and voted that I should be excused the customary payments, which would have amounted to twenty-five guineas; and ever since have given me their *Transactions* gratis. They also presented me with the gold medal of Sir Godfrey Copley for the year 1753, the delivery of which was accompanied by a very handsome speech of the president, Lord Macclesfield, wherein I was highly honored. . . .

FRANKLIN AS SEEN BY TWO CONTEMPORARIES

George Washington: A PHILOSOPHIC MIND

TO BENJAMIN FRANKLIN

New York, September 23, 1789.

DEAR Sir: The affectionate congratulations on the recovery of my health, and the warm expressions of personal friendship which were contained in your favor of the 16th instant,* claim my gratitude. And the consideration that it was written when you were afflicted with a painful malady, greatly increases my obligation for it.

Would to God, my dear Sir, that I could congratulate you upon the removal of that excruciating pain under which you

* Franklin had written: "For my own personal Ease, I should have died two years ago; but tho' those Years have been spent in excruciating Pain, I am pleas'd that I have liv'd them, since they have brought me to see our present Situation. I am now finishing my 84th. [year] and probably with it my Career in this Life; but in what ever State of Existence I am plac'd hereafter, if I retain any Memory of what has pass'd here, I shall with it retain the Esteem, Respect, and Affection with which I have long been, my dear Friend, Yours most sincerely."

labour! and that your existence might close with as much ease to yourself, as its continuance has been beneficial to our Country and useful to mankind! Or, if the United wishes of a free people, joined with the earnest prayers of every friend to Science and humanity could relieve the body from pains or infirmities, you could claim an exemption on this score. But this cannot be, and you have within yourself the only resource to which we can confidently apply for relief: a *Philosophic mind.*

If to be venerated for benevolence: If to be admired for talents: If to be esteemed for patriotism: if to be beloved for philanthropy, can gratify the human mind, you must have the pleasing consolation to know that you have not lived in vain; And I flatter myself that it will not be ranked among the least grateful occurrences of your life to be assured that so long as I retain my memory, you will be thought on with respect, veneration and Affection by Your sincere friend etc.

From John C. Fitzpatrick, ed., *The Writings of George Washington* (Washington: Government Printing Office, 1939), XXX, 409.

John Adams: AN EXAGGERATED REPUTATION

Franklin's moral character can neither be applauded nor condemned, without discrimination and many limitations.

To all those talents and qualities for the foundation of a great and lasting character, which were held up to the view of

the whole world by the university of Oxford, the Royal Society of London, and the Royal Academy of Sciences in Paris, were added, it is believed, more artificial modes of diffusing, celebrating, and exaggerating his reputation, than were ever

From Charles Francis Adams, *The Works of John Adams* (Boston: Little, Brown and Company, 1856), I, 660–664.

before or since practised in favor of any individual. . . .

His reputation was more universal than that of Leibnitz or Newton, Frederick or Voltaire, and his character more beloved and esteemed than any or all of them. Newton had astonished perhaps forty or fifty men in Europe; for not more than that number, probably, at any one time had read him and understood him by his discoveries and demonstrations. And these being held in admiration in their respective countries as at the head of the philosophers, had spread among scientific people a mysterious wonder at the genius of this perhaps the greatest man that ever lived. But this fame was confined to men of letters. The common people knew little and cared nothing about such a recluse philosopher. Leibnitz's name was more confined still. Frederick was hated by more than half of Europe as much as Louis the Fourteenth was, and as Napoleon is. Voltaire, whose name was more universal than any of those before mentioned, was considered as a vain, profligate wit, and not much esteemed or beloved by anybody, though admired by all who knew his works. But Franklin's fame was universal. His name was familiar to government and people, to kings, courtiers, nobility, clergy, and philosophers, as well as plebeians, to such a degree that there was scarcely a peasant or a citizen, a *valet de chambre*, coachman or footman, a lady's chambermaid or a scullion in a kitchen, who was not familiar with it, and who did not consider him as a friend to human kind. When they spoke of him, they seemed to think he was to restore the golden age. . . . To develop that complication of causes, which conspired to produce so singular a phenomenon, is far beyond my means or forces. Perhaps it can never be done without a complete history of the philosophy and politics of the eight-

eenth century. . . . Without going back to Lord Herbert, to Hobbes, to Mandeville, or to a host of more obscure infidels, both in England, France, and Germany, it is enough to say that four of the finest writers that Great Britain ever produced, Shaftesbury, Bolingbroke, Hume, and Gibbon, whose labors were translated into all languages, and three of the most eloquent writers that ever lived in France, whose works were also translated into all languages, Voltaire, Rousseau, and Raynal, seem to have made it the study of their lives and the object of their most strenuous exertions, to render mankind in Europe discontented with their situation in life, and with the state of society, both in religion and government. Princes and courtiers as well as citizens and countrymen, clergy as well as laity, became infected. The King of Prussia, the Empress Catherine, were open and undisguised. The Emperor Joseph the Second was suspected, and even the excellent and amiable King of France grew impatient and uneasy under the fatiguing ceremonies of the Catholic church. All these and many more were professed admirers of Mr. Franklin. . . .

He had been educated a printer, and had practised his art in Boston, Philadelphia, and London for many years, where he not only learned the full power of the press to exalt and to spread a man's fame, but acquired the intimacy and the correspondence of many men of that profession, with all their editors and many of their correspondents. This whole tribe became enamoured and proud of Mr. Franklin as a member of their body, and were consequently always ready and eager to publish and embellish any panegyric upon him that they could procure. . . .

While he had the singular felicity to enjoy the entire esteem and affection of all the philosophers of every denomination, he was not less regarded by all the sects and denominations of Christians. The Catholics thought him almost a Catholic. The Church of England claimed him as one of them. The Presbyterians thought him half a Presbyterian, and the Friends believed him a wet Quaker. The dissenting clergymen in England and America were among the most distinguished asserters and propagators of his renown. Indeed, all sects considered him, and I believe justly, a friend to unlimited toleration in matters of religion.

Nothing, perhaps, that ever occurred upon this earth was so well calculated to give any man an extensive and universal celebrity as the discovery of the efficacy of iron points and the invention of lightning-rods. The idea was one of the most sublime that ever entered a human imagination, that a mortal should disarm the clouds of heaven, and almost "snatch from his hand the sceptre and the rod." The ancients would have enrolled him with Bacchus and Ceres, Hercules and Minerva. His *Paratonnères* erected their heads in all parts of the world, on temples and palaces no less than on cottages of peasants and the habitations of ordinary citizens. These visible objects reminded all men of the name and character of their inventor; and, in the course of time, have not only tranquillized the minds, and dissipated the fears of the tender sex and their timorous children, but have almost annihilated that panic terror and superstitious horror which was once almost universal in violent storms of thunder and lightning. To condense all the rays of this glory to a focus, to sum it up in a single line, to impress it on every mind and transmit it to all posterity, a motto was devised for his picture, and soon became familiar to the memory of every schoolboy who understood a word of Latin:

"Eripuit cœlo fulmen sceptrumque tyrannis."[1]

Thus it appeared at first, and the author of it was held in a mysterious obscurity. But, after some time, M. Turgot altered it to

"Eripuit cœlo fulmen; mox sceptra tyrannis."[2]

By the first line, the rulers of Great Britain and their arbitrary oppressions of the Colonies were alone understood. By the second was intimated that Mr. Franklin was soon to destroy or at least to dethrone all kings and abolish all monarchical governments. This, it cannot be disguised, flattered at that time the ruling popular passion of all Europe. . . .

The general discontents in Europe have not been produced by any increase of the power of kings, for monarchical authority has been greatly diminished in all parts of Europe during the last century, but by the augmentation of the wealth and power of the aristocracies. The great and general extension of commerce has introduced such inequalities of property, that the class of middling people, that great and excellent portion of society upon whom so much of the liberty and prosperity of nations so greatly depends, is almost lost; and the two orders of rich and poor only remain. By this means kings have fallen more into the power and under the direction of the aristocracies, and the middle classes, upon whom kings chiefly depended for support against the encroachments of the nobles and the rich, have failed. The people find themselves burdened now by the rich, and by the power of the crown now commonly wielded by the rich. And as knowledge

[1] "He snatched the lightning from the sky and the sceptre from tyrants."

[2] "As he has wrested the lightning from heaven, so he would soon wrest the sceptre from tyrants."

and education, ever since the Reformation, have been increasing among the common people, they feel their burdens more sensibly, grow impatient under them, and more desirous of throwing them off. The immense revenues of the church, the crowns, and all the great proprietors of land, the armies and navies must all be paid by the people, who groan and stagger under the weight. The few who think and see the progress and tendency of things, have long foreseen that resistance in some shape or other must be resorted to, some time or other. They have not been able to see any resource but in the common people; indeed, in republicanism, and that republicanism must be democracy; because the whole power of the aristocracy, as of the monarchies, aided by the church, must be wielded against them. Hence the popularity of all insurrections against the ordinary authority of government during the last century. Hence the popularity of Pascal Paoli, the Polish insurrections, the American Revolution, and the present struggle in Spain and Portugal. When, where, and in what manner all this will end, God only knows. To this cause Mr. Franklin owed much of his popularity. He was considered to be in his heart no friend to kings, nobles, or prelates. He was thought a profound legislator, and a friend of democracy. He was thought to be the magician who had excited the ignorant Americans to resistance. His mysterious wand had separated the Colonies from Great Britain. He had framed and established all the American constitutions of government, especially all the best of them, *i.e.* the most democratical. His plans and his example were to abolish monarchy, aristocracy, and hierarchy throughout the world. Such opinions as these were entertained by the Duke de la Rochefoucauld, M. Turgot, M. Condorcet, and a thousand other men of learning and eminence in France, England, Holland, and all the rest of Europe.

Mr. Franklin, however, after all, and notwithstanding all his faults and errors, was a great and eminent benefactor to his country and mankind.

Such was the real character, and so much more formidable was the artificial character of Dr. Franklin, . . .

Franklin had a great genius, original, sagacious, and inventive, capable of discoveries in science no less than of improvements in the fine arts and the mechanic arts. He had a vast imagination, equal to the comprehension of the greatest objects, and capable of a steady and cool comprehension of them. He had wit at will. He had humor that, when he pleased, was delicate and delightful. He had a satire that was good-natured or caustic, Horace or Juvenal, Swift or Rabelais, at his pleasure. He had talents for irony, allegory, and fable, that he could adapt with great skill to the promotion of moral and political truth. He was master of that infantine simplicity which the French call *naïveté*, which never fails to charm, in Phaedrus and La Fontaine, from the cradle to the grave. Had he been blessed with the same advantages of scholastic education in his early youth, and pursued a course of studies as unembarrassed with occupations of public and private life, as Sir Isaac Newton, he might have emulated the first philosopher. Although I am not ignorant that most of his positions and hypotheses have been controverted, I cannot but think he has added much to the mass of natural knowledge, and contributed largely to the progress of the human mind, both by his own writings and by the controversies and experiments he has excited in all parts of Europe. He had abilities for investigating statistical questions, and in some parts of his life has written pamphlets and essays upon public topics with great ingenuity and success; but after my acquaintance with him, which commenced in congress in 1775, his excellence as a legislator, a politician, or a negotiator most certainly never appeared. No sentiment more weak and superficial was ever avowed by the most absurd philosopher than some of his, particularly one that he procured to be inserted in the first constitution of Pennsylvania, and for which he had such a fondness as to insert it in his will.[3] I call it weak, for so it must have been, or hypocritical; unless he meant by one satiric touch to ridicule his own republic, or throw it into everlasting contempt.

I must acknowledge, after all, that nothing in life has mortified or grieved me more than the necessity which compelled me to oppose him so often as I have. He was a man with whom I always wished to live in friendship, and for that purpose omitted no demonstration of respect, esteem, and veneration in my power, until I had unequivocal proofs of

[3] The reference is to the following line in the Codicil to Franklin's will: "It having long been a fixed political opinion of mine, that in a democratical state there ought to be no offices of profit, for the reasons I had given in an article of my drawing in our Constitution, it was my intention when I accepted the office of President [of Pennsylvania], to devote the appointed salary to some public uses." ED.

his hatred, for no other reason under the sun, but because I gave my judgment in opposition to his, in many points which materially affected the interests of our country, and in many more which essentially concerned our happiness, safety, and well-being. I could not and would not sacrifice the clearest dictates of my understanding and the purest principles of morals and policy in compliance to Dr. Franklin. When historians shall hereafter inform posterity that Mr. Adams was not beloved by his venerable colleague, it is to be hoped that they will explain this truth by adding, that Mr. Izard, Mr. Lee, Mr. Dana, and many other honest patriots were not beloved by him, and that Mr. Silas Deane and many others of his stamp were beloved by him.

What shall we do with these gentlemen of great souls and vast views, who, without the least tincture of vanity, *bonâ fide* believe themselves the greatest men in the world, fully qualified and clearly entitled to govern their governors and command their commanders as well as their equals and inferiors, purely for their good and without the smallest interest for themselves? Though it may be true, as Dr. Young says, proud as this world is, there is more superiority in it given than assumed, yet it is certain there is sometimes more assumed than the world is willing to give. Such, unfortunately for Dr. Franklin, was his destiny . . .

Carl Van Doren: MEET DOCTOR FRANKLIN

SINCE I have at one time or other spoken about so many aspects of Franklin to so many groups in Philadelphia I may not be able to avoid some repetitions this afternoon, but I will do

what I can to avoid it. At this opening talk of this interesting series I shall have to be a little more discursive than some of the more systematic speakers who come later.

From "Meet Dr. Franklin" by Carl Van Doren in *Meet Dr. Franklin* (Philadelphia: The Franklin Institute, 1943), pp. 1–10. Used by permission of the publishers.

Franklin had, I think, the most eminent mind that has ever existed in America. No wonder there are so many legendary misconceptions of him that it is difficult now to restore and comprehend him in the great integrity of his mind, character, and personality. He appears, somehow, to be a syndicate of men. We study him as a scientist, as a diplomat, as a statesman, as a business man, as an economist, as a printer, as a humorist and wit, as a great writer, as a sage, and as a landmark in the history of human speech about the common ways of life. What had been said before he so often said better. He was great in friendship, and in his later years was probably the most renowned private citizen on earth. It has recently been more than once remarked — and printed — that Benjamin Franklin was the American Leonardo da Vinci. This is American modesty, if not colonialism. Why not occasionally say that Leonard da Vinci was the Italian Benjamin Franklin?

Franklin was the earliest American whom, without limiting ourselves to national terms, we can call a very great man. When you try to define his particular greatness you run into what John Adams felt in his jealous days in Paris. Adams was a great man, but not a very great man. A great man such as Adams living with a very great man such as Franklin cannot tell the difference between himself and the other. Adams could not tell why people thought the difference to be so enormous. Nor can anybody express the difference better than with a fairly common, if not entirely just, geographical analogy. Imagine yourself in a range of mountains. You look up, and several of the mountains seem to you, from where you stand, as high as the master of them all. But when you get to a distance which gives perspective you see that the great mountain towers above the others, which

are, in a sense, only foothills to it. This was true of many men with whom Franklin was associated during his life, who were as far from being aware of his genuine superiority as posterity has sometimes been since then. Moreover, his superiority is the hardest kind to measure. We can sometimes measure superiority when it shows itself in outward acts, achievements, tumults, benefits, or damages. Franklin's eminence was in his almost supreme mind that moved to its countless tasks with what seems perfect ease. Both the supremacy and the ease are hard for us to explain because they are so nearly unique in history that comparisons fail us. And without comparisons there can be no measurements.

There are, of course, people who take an attitude toward Franklin that may remind us of the fate of Aristides. For his virtues, you will remember, he had a peevish vote cast against him by an illiterate man who was tired of hearing Aristides called Aristides the Just. We often have an impulse to fear and distrust great excellence. We say we like it, but in our hearts we suspect it of being more — and consequently less — than human. When we say this or that hero is "human" we always mean he is weak in some way that is comforting. All of us are weak, and we like to believe this is human of us. When we find a similar weakness in a great man we are pleased because it means that the great are not so much greater than we are after all.

It is now and then asked if Franklin did not get most or many of his ideas from other men, and then out of vanity take the credit to himself. I do not think Franklin was particularly vain. In the third paragraph of his Autobiography he disarmingly admitted that telling his story might gratify his vanity. "Most people dislike vanity in others, whatever share they have of it themselves; but I give it quarter wherever I meet with it, being persuaded that it is often productive of good to its possessor, and to others that are within his sphere of action; and therefore, in many cases, it would not be altogether absurd if a man were to thank God for his vanity among the other comforts of life." Franklin knew that the false modesty which men conventionally affect is a mode of self-conscious egotism.

What could Franklin do when he wrote his Autobiography but tell of things he had done or helped do? Why should he have talked as with his hand over his mouth or his elbow over his head? Everybody knew he was great and famous. For him to pretend not to know that would have been silly, a form of stage fright. In a letter about the classic epigram of Turgot which said Franklin had snatched the lightning from the sky and the scepter from tyrants, Franklin in 1781 honestly protested. "It ascribes too much to me, especially in what relates to the tyrant; the Revolution having been the work of many able and brave men, wherein it is sufficient honor for me if I am allowed a small share."

Or go back to an earlier year in Franklin's life, when he was not so famous and might have been tempted not to be so generous. In the fall of 1753 he got together what he called a "philosophical packet" of letters exchanged between him and various scientific friends of his in America. It was an important year for Franklin. The king of France had complimented the remote Philadelphia tradesman on his electrical discoveries, Harvard and Yale had given him honorary degrees, the Royal Society in November awarded him the Copley gold medal. The "philosophical packet" was to signalize what Franklin hoped would be a fresh beginning for him in the scientific career he

looked forward to. Among these papers was a letter from James Bowdoin of Boston, dated November 12, in which he — before any other scientist so far as is known — hit on the first true explanation of "luminosity" (phosphorescence) in sea water: "that the said appearance might be caused by a great number of little animals, floating on the surface of the sea, which, on being disturbed, might, by expanding their finns, or otherwise moving themselves, expose such a part of their bodies as exhibits a luminous appearance, somewhat in the manner of a glow-worm, or fire-fly."

Here was a subject Franklin had already speculated on. He had at first conjectured that this luminosity was "owing to electric fire, produced by friction between the particles of water and those of salt. Living far from the sea, I had then no opportunity of making experiments on the sea water, and so embraced this opinion too hastily. For in 1750 and 1751, being occasionally on the sea coast, I found, by experiments, that sea water in a bottle, though at first it would by agitation appear luminous, yet in a few hours it lost that virtue; hence, and from this . . . I first began to doubt of my former hypothesis, and to suspect that the luminous appearance in sea water must be owing to some other principles."

Bowdoin's conjecture at once struck Franklin as sounder than his own. "It is indeed very possible," he wrote in a letter dated 13 December, "that an extremely small animalcule, too small to be visible even by the best glasses, may yet give a visible light. I remember to have taken notice, in a drop of kennel water magnified by the solar microscope to the bigness of a cart-wheel, there were numbers of visible animalcules swimming about; but I was sure there were likewise some which I could not see, even with that magnifier; for the wake they made in swimming to and fro was very visible, though the body that made it was not so. Now, if I could see the wake of an invisible animalcule, I imagine I might much more easily see its light if it were of the luminous kind. For how small is the extent of a ship's wake, compared with that of the light of her lantern."

Dr. Edwin Grant Conklin of the American Philosophical Society recently told me that a Japanese scholar had called Franklin's comment on these animalcules in sea water the earliest guess at the existence and nature of the microörganisms, as we should now call them, which are responsible for the phenomenon. Franklin had nothing to do with the error. He kept back his own letter (to be published long after his death), and sent Bowdoin's to London, where it was read before the Royal Society in December 1756 and later included in the 1769 edition of Franklin's "Experiments and Observations on Electricity," as "a Letter from J. B. Esq.; in Boston, to B. F. concerning the Light in Sea-Water." The credit was Bowdoin's, and Franklin plainly gave it to him.

This same 1769 volume, among the most fascinating in the whole range of eighteenth-century "philosophical" writings, punctiliously credited Thomas Hopkinson, Ebenezer Kinnersley, and Philip Syng with their original suggestions and discoveries made during the "Philadelphia experiments." If the three came to be overlooked in the light of their greater colleague, it was hardly Franklin's fault. Reporting to Peter Collinson in London, Franklin constantly spoke of "our electrical enquiries" and the things "we" had found out, never pretending to have done the work alone. The first collection of his "Experiments and Observations" (1751) was possibly printed in London before Franklin in Philadelphia had known it

was to be. Because he alone had written the reports, his name alone was given on the title-page. In his own copy of the pamphlet he marked each experiment with the initials of the discoverer: Hopkinson's once, Kinnersley's seven times and once jointly with Franklin's, Syng's three times. There can be little doubt that Franklin was always chief among the experimenters, as there can be none that he was the best writer among them. But he did not make excessive claims for himself. What happened was that as he went on growing more and more famous, the world credited him with more and more achievements, past as well as present. In the world at large, first men are dramatically first, and the rest nowhere to speak of.

I know it is commonly said that the Autobiography is a retouched photograph in which Franklin emphasizes his own share in the life of his times and minimizes that of other men. I also know that I have spent many days and weeks investigating this very matter and have come to the conclusion that he left out things he had done more often than he even seemed to claim to have done things he had not. Philadelphia during the great years of the Junto (1727 to 1757) was a town of remarkable intellectual activity, and its history has not yet been truly written as I hope it will some day be. But no matter what claims may be made for other men, Franklin emerges as the chief among them, the energizing, galvanizing source of two-thirds of the town's important enterprises.

When I am told, as I occasionally am, that I make Franklin out as larger than life, I can only answer that Franklin must have been what he was, because nobody could have invented such a figure. Stranger things happen in fact than in fiction. Nature is richer in invention than men are. The great characters in fiction are almost always heroes who have each of them some ruling passion, with enough human weaknesses to give him a reasonable credibility. Romantic creation is most likely to be exaggeration along a few lines. But the more you study Franklin the more lines you find running out from him in all directions, and the more facts that no poet — however romantic and exaggerative — would ever have thought of inventing. The wonder of Franklin is the facts that are true about him. The more exact the research into his character, the more surprising the adventure.

Too much emphasis has been laid, I think, on his simple practical ingenuities. You go into a grocer's and see the clerk taking objects down from high shelves with a device based on the "long arm" which Franklin invented to get at his books. Most of us have in our kitchens a combination chair-and-stepladder which Franklin seems to have devised; and in our fireplaces a draft such as he had made for his fireplace in Craven Street. He has been credited with the invention of the rocking chair, which I believe he did not invent, though in his last years he had one which automatically fanned him when he rocked. But the ingenuity that went into these gadgets is less notable than the fundamental ideas behind Franklin's principal inventions.

If, for example, we read his remarkable pamphlet about what he called the Pennsylvania fireplace, later known as the Franklin stove, we should not be too much taken by the salesmanlike adroitness of his arguments. It is true he was adroit, particularly in his claims that the use of the stove would be beneficial to the health, complexion, and beauty of women. Such arguments were as likely to be effective in 1744 as they would be

in 1939. But Franklin believed they were sound, as they were. He had not designed his stove purely for economy in fuel. He had strongly in mind the great importance of proper ventilation, and its value for health. He even took into account an esthetic element. His stove, unlike the Dutch and German stoves of the time, allowed people to see the fire, "which is in itself a pleasant thing." In 1744 Franklin had been using his stove, he said, for "the four winters past," which takes the invention back to 1740. But he put off writing about it till he had announced the organization of the American Philosophical Society. His pamphlet was in effect his first contribution to the work of this new league of scientists. As if to give his little treatise the dignity of learning, he accompanied it with notes from various impressive sources, one of them in Latin.

Certainly the lightning-rod was not a gadget. The experiment which Franklin proposed, to prove whether electricity and lightning were identical, and his own separate demonstration with the kite, must be ranked with the most fundamental as well as the most striking experiments in scientific history. The story of the kite is now so old and so familiar that it has come to seem a pleasant legend, not much more real to us than the customary pictures of the scene, which show Franklin's son as a little boy when in fact he was twenty-one or so and as tall as his father. The experiment, because it solved a mystery, has so deprived lightning of its terror that it no longer overawes men. Franklin, drawing the lightning from the skies, removed it from the dread region of mythology. Kant was not speaking for picturesque effect when he said Franklin was a new Prometheus who had stolen fire from heaven. The expression meant, literally, that Franklin had made men equals of the gods and therefore free of an ancient slavish dread. Nobody in 1752 felt that the kite story was a quaint little incident. It was something immense, and it gave Franklin the reputation of a wizard, not too much unlike Merlin or Roger Bacon — or, in our day, Einstein.

I have, I suppose, already made it clear that I do not agree with those almost unanimous modern commentators on Franklin who think of him as primarily an ingenious inventor. I will go further and say that I think his fundamental conjectures are more important than his inventions. He said of himself: "I own I have too strong a penchant to the building of hypotheses; they indulge my natural indolence." But these hypotheses were as truly original as anything he ever invented. What he called his "conjectures and suppositions" about electricity make up the Principia of the science. Nor did he confine himself to one branch of science, or to science as a whole. His notes in 1743 on the origin of northeast storms were the first step toward a scientific meteorology. In his "Observations Concerning the Increase of Mankind, Peopling of Countries, etc.," written in 1751, he not only anticipated Malthus, who acknowledged his debt to Franklin, but also forecast the theory of the American frontier later associated with the name of Frederick Jackson Turner. In 1754 Franklin in his famous letters to Governor Shirley of Massachusetts set down his far-sighted plan for equal justice to the various parts of the British Empire, and summed up almost all the American arguments of the Revolution. In 1762 he wrote the earliest piece of scientific musical criticism, and in 1768 said as much as has been said since about the need of reform in English spelling. He was the first scholar who studied the Gulf Stream (1769) and had some understanding of it and the possible use of it by navigators; and among the first who insisted that the common cold is more likely to come from contagion than from exposure. As he put it in one of the notes he made 1773 for a paper he intended to write: "Think they get cold by coming *out* of such hot rooms; they get them by being *in*."

Though from 1773 to 1783 Franklin was so much absorbed in politics he had little time for general ideas, he had hardly signed the final treaty of peace with England when his mind was alert with bold conjectures again. Having seen the first ascent of human passengers in a free balloon, in Paris in November 1783, Franklin at once — and apparently alone among his contemporaries — foresaw the possibility of aerial warfare. This discovery, he wrote in December, might "give a new turn to human affairs. Convincing sovereigns of the folly of wars may perhaps be one effect of it; since it will be impossible for the most potent of them to guard his dominions. Five thousand balloons, capable of raising two men each, would not cost more than five ships of the line; and where is the prince who can afford so to cover his country with troops for its defence as that ten thousand men descending from the clouds might not in many places do an infinite deal of mischief before a force could be brought together to repel them?" As I speak armed forces in Europe are each hesitating to attack for fear of the very consequences Franklin foresaw at a glance.

Franklin's own age knew him as philosopher and sage, statesman and wit, and while delighting in his charm and grace thought of him as always a figure of weight and dignity. It remained for another century to take affectionate familiarities with him, and call him Ben Franklin — which only his immediate family ever did — as the century called other heroes Andy Jackson and Abe Lincoln. The homely anecdotes of Franklin's Autobiography gave him a homespun reputation which does him less than justice. There was little that was shirt-sleeved in his science or politics or diplomacy. His manners as I have written elsewhere, "were as urbane and expert as his prose." His economical maxims give a wrong impression of his character, which was generous and at times lavish. "Avarice and happiness never saw each other," he wrote as Poor Richard. "How then should they become acquainted?" So far from making a great virtue of the cunning which has been often ascribed to him, Franklin as Poor Richard said that "Cunning proceeds from want of capacity"— meaning that truth was better. "Dr. Franklin," Henry Laurens wrote when the British ministers were warily looking for some one to treat with Franklin for peace in 1782, "knows very well how to manage a cunning man; but when the Doctor converses or treats with a man of candor there is no man more candid than himself."

Though Franklin was an excellent and successful business man, he retired from active business at forty-two and spent forty-two years more in the service of the public. He might have made a fortune if he had patented his stove or his lightning-rod. He refused to patent anything which he thought might be of benefit to mankind. As he did not hungrily gather wealth, so he did not cautiously guard his comfort or safety. It must never be forgotten that in his seventieth year Franklin might with decency have done what his more conservative son advised him to do: that is, retire from active affairs and let younger men settle the conflict between England and America. Instead Franklin, at the risk of peace and even of his neck, took his stand with the revolutionaries. Life with him began all over again at seventy. The older the bolder.

I shall take the liberty of reading the final words of my "Benjamin Franklin," in which I have done my best to reduce his qualities to their essence. "Franklin was not one of those men who owe their greatness merely to the opportunities of their times. In any age, in any place, Franklin would have been great. Mind and will, talent and art, strength and ease, wit and grace met in him as if nature had been lavish and happy when he was shaped. Nothing seems to have been left out except a passionate desire, as in most men of genius, to be all ruler, all soldier, all saint, all poet, all scholar, all some one gift or merit or success. Franklin's powers were from first to last in a flexible equilibrium. Even his genius could not specialize him. He moved through his world in a humorous mastery of it. Kind as he was, there was perhaps a little contempt in his lack of exigency. He could not put so high a value as single-minded men put on the things they give their lives for. Possessions were not worth that much, nor achievements. Comfortable as Franklin's possessions and numerous as his achievements were, they were less than he was. Whoever learns about his deeds remembers longest the man who did them. And sometimes, with his marvelous range, in spite of his personal tang, he seems to have been more than any single man: a harmonious human multitude."

Frank Davidson: THREE PATTERNS OF LIVING

A SCIENTIST asserted in a recent number of the *Bulletin* of the American Association of University Professors that "our real job as teachers" is "to cultivate a well-balanced appreciation of values, to teach what is most worth while in life and how to go about to achieve it."[1] Walt Whitman once spoke of the acquisition of appreciation of values as prudence and clarified his peculiar meaning of the word with a line suggestive of the Scriptures, "that the young man who composedly periled his life and lost it has done exceeding well for himself, while the man who has not periled his life and retains it to old age in riches and ease has perhaps achieved nothing for himself worth mentioning." Centuries ago Jesus gave a lesson in the appreciation of values in his parable of the Good Samaritan, the Levite, and the Priest. "Which of these three," he asked, "thinkest thou, was neighbor unto him that fell among the thieves?" The scientist, Whitman, and Jesus properly imply values beyond the material ones. And our experiences daily testify to the truth of their implications.

With these observations in mind, let us project a problem in values. Jonathan Edwards, Benjamin Franklin, and John Woolman, three eighteenth century Americans, each left an autobiographical statement expressive of his personal pattern of living. What is the relative value of their contributions to those of us who are interested in "what is most worth

[1] C. Judson Herrick, "A Liberal Education," Autumn, 1945, Vol. 31, No. 3, p. 356.

while in life" and who would know "how to go about to achieve it"?

II

Jonathan Edwards, born in 1703, was of the Connecticut pulpit aristocracy. He was a man of culture. A prodigy of learning and of logical thinking, he was writing scientific essays at twelve. He kept an interest in science — biological and psychological — throughout his life, but always in a position subordinate to that of theology and religion. Both his scientific and his religious bents made him sympathetic with the natural world about him. To some extent it was revelatory of God, though it was not God. After one particular experience he expressed his insight into nature as a poet might, suggesting a beauty there beyond the merely physical.

God's excellence [he muses], his wisdom, his purity and love, seemed to appear in every thing; in the sun, moon, and stars; in the clouds, and blue sky; in the grass, flowers, trees; in the water, and all nature; which used greatly to fix my mind. . . . And scarce any thing, among all the works of nature was so delightful to me as thunder and lightning; formerly, nothing had been so terrible to me. Before, I used to be uncommonly terrified with thunder, and to be struck with terror when I saw a thunder storm rising; but now, on the contrary, it rejoiced me. I felt God, so to speak, at the first appearance of a thunder storm; and used to take the opportunity, at such times, to fix myself in order to view the clouds, and see the lightning play, and hear the majestic and awful voice of God's thunder. . . .

Reprinted with permission from the *Bulletin*, American Association of University Professors, Volume 34 (Summer, 1948), pp. 364–374.

As one might surmise from the passage, Edwards had an interest in esthetics — in both the theoretical and practical phases. Disturbed while still a youth by the terms *ugly* and *beautiful,* as men applied them to objects, he studied to learn the basis of such differentiation. By designs of his own creation he discovered that proportion was a fundamental factor, but still he was not satisfied. He would know why things properly proportioned affect the mind as beautiful and the disproportioned as ugly. His investigation led him at length to the inference that proportion is characteristic of Being, that disproportion is a negation of Being. In his writing he employed artistic devices that make for effective communication. Even in such a theological monstrosity as *Sinners in the Hands of an Angry God* he is powerful, and stimulates one's sense of beauty through his logic, his rhythmic repetition of motives, his simple figures, and his direct appeal. He employs these devices, as a painter might use line and color, to focus the reader's attention on the man who, steeped in sin, hangs by a slender thread over a bottomless pit.

His greatest fault, perhaps, lay in his permitting himself to be deflected from his idealistic and mystical consideration of life to become, in such sermons, a defender of Puritan theology. But Arminianism and Deism, which for him were but rationalizings instead of faiths, were making inroads on the religion of the fathers. Since by training he had the logical method that belongs to an advocate, he spoke, though temperamentally he was not fitted for the task. Nor was he religiously. For he had proceeded as far beyond doctrinal Calvinism as Emerson in 1833 had beyond doctrinal Unitarianism.

His strength lay in his idealism and in his mysticism; and by what he suggests to us in these fields he should be remembered. As idealist he developed views similar to those of his English contemporary Berkeley. The physical universe was for him but an idea of God made manifest to man. Reality was in the idea rather than in the manifestation, even as reality of one of our thoughts is in the thought rather than in its spoken or written form. Emerson, later, found the view attractive and gave a chapter to idealism in his essay *Nature.* Our own contemplation of that view might be a corrective today for a too rampant materialism. At one point in his discussion of Being, Edwards stated "that those beings, which have knowledge and consciousness, are the only proper and real, and substantial beings; inasmuch as the being of other things is only by these. From hence, we may see the gross mistake of those, who think material things the only substantial beings. . . ."

He was, as I have said, a mystic; that is, he had a sense at times of being in the immediate presence of deity, of undergoing for the moment an experience that had a reality not given by sensory contact with a material environment, of knowing a spiritual ecstasy that was beyond words to express. Here is his own account:

Once as I rode out into the woods for my health, in 1737, having alighted from my horse in a retired place, as my manner commonly has been, to walk for divine contemplation and prayer, I had a view that for me was extraordinary, of the glory of the Son of God, as Mediator between God and Man, and his wonderful, great, full, pure and sweet grace and love, and meek and gentle condescension. This grace that appeared so calm and sweet, appeared also great above the heavens. The person of Christ appeared ineffably excellent with an excellency great enough to swallow up all thought and conception — which continued, as near as I can judge, about an hour . . .

I am not a mystic; nor am I one to say

that the mystic's experience is not a valid one. If we come forward a century from this confession of Edwards, we find a somewhat parallel one in Emerson:

Standing on this bare ground [he says], — my head bathed by the blithe air, and uplifted into infinite space, — all mean egotism vanishes. I become a transparent eyeball; I am nothing; I see all; the currents of the Universal Being circulate through me; I am part or parcel of God.

"To the sceptic," says a modern Emersonian scholar,

all mysticism will seem to be, more than likely, only one more illusion. And one more illusion it may be. Or it may be, potentially, a deepening and extension of the conscious life beyond the familiar limits, a veritable enrichment of experience which the sceptic may reasonably take cognizance of and consider. He can do so, however, only at first hand. For mysticism, really to be known, must be known from within.

In any evaluation of Edwards with reference to "what is most worth while in life" we must keep in mind the mystic Edwards. And remembering what mystics have contributed to man's cultural heritage — Teresa of Avila, Catherine of Siena, Robert Southwell, William Blake, William Wordsworth, Ralph Waldo Emerson, Francis Thompson, and William Vaughn Moody — we must not dismiss too hastily the Connecticut Puritan.

Though sympathetic with the medieval manner of exalting the spirit and abasing the flesh, Edwards was not ascetic. He functioned as a tutor at Yale; fell in love, married, and reared a large family; preached for a quarter century at Northampton; labored as a missionary among the Indians in western Massachusetts; and shortly before his death accepted

appointment to the Presidency of the College of New Jersey.

He was logical and profound in his thinking, idealistic, deeply spiritual and devout, mystical — capable of making men realize that they are more in their composition than what shows between hat and boot soles. He is reminiscent of that strain in human thought which produced *Everyman*, "My Mind to Me a Kingdom Is," and "Litany in Time of Plague." It may be summarized in Nashe's lines:

> Heaven is our heritage
> Earth but a player's stage.

III

Benjamin Franklin, born three years later than Edwards, was of a family that for generations had lived by the sweat of its brow. He was reared in a faith similar to that of Edwards but was so attracted by the physical scene about him as to adapt himself quickly to it and its ways. Like his ancestors for generations back, he was bred to a trade through a long apprenticeship. That he became a journalist was not altogether accident. His Uncle Benjamin and his maternal grandfather had been versifiers, and his elder brother had become printer of the fourth newspaper set up in New England. Moreover, he learned early that writing, if one has a mastery of it, is useful for creating and controlling the opinions of men. The story of his teaching himself to write is generally known. The motive was utilitarian. While in epistolary controversy with a friend, Collins, he showed his father some of the letters that had passed between them and was warned that, though he had the better ideas, Collins was winning through the advantage of effective form. So, Franklin made brief notes on paragraphs from the *Spectator*, cast the items of his outlines into disorder, and then, when he had forgot the words of his model, tried recasting the paragraphs. He could compare his with the originals. He reached a stage in his progress where he thought that his expression was at times an improvement on Addison's.

He came to be a writer of power in his appeal to men's intelligence. He never loses poise or control. But he seldom, if ever, stirs the emotions. With the exception of the *Autobiography,* which is charming in its seeming artlessness, his writing is marked by cleverness, wit, grace, charm, lucidity, urbanity, and irony. Of the last he became a master. In his pointed essay on *Rules by Which a Great Empire May Be Reduced* he sets up a ridiculous objective (that one would want to reduce his empire); then he states with great economy twenty rules – all facts concerning British colonial policy – by which such an end may be attained. The implication is, of course, that the action of the English ministry is ridiculous. But whether the writing be a satire directed at a tyrannical government or a charming bagatelle addressed to Madame Helvétius, it has an enameled surface – smooth, glistening, durable, useful. For better or for worse, Franklin seldom leads a reader beyond depth.

His accomplishments through his eighty-four years are known in many languages. He invented a stove, bifocals, and lightning rods – all useful. He reorganized the British Post Office in America, put it on a paying basis, and through it helped to unify the colonies. He established a city police system, an efficient city fire control, a public hospital, and a subscription library, and helped materially in laying the foundation of the University of Pennsylvania. He organized a defense for his colony when it was threatened by the French and Indians,

took a force of men to a wilderness frontier near Bethlehem and there directed the building of three forts, offered a plan of union for the colonies at the Albany Congress – a plan that he later thought, had it been adopted, might have prevented the Revolution, and, by collecting wagons, horses, drivers, and food supplies, made possible Braddock's tragic expedition into the back country with British troops. Then he served as diplomat in England and France for twenty-five years, as a member of the committee which drew the Declaration of Independence, and as a delegate to the Constitutional Convention. And these are but major items in his accomplishments.

He was no mystic, as was Edwards; nor was he spiritually minded. He supported the church as he supported other public institutions – because it had a social value and because supporting it had a social value. He had swung off on the bias of Deism in his youth, but had forsaken the course for practical reasons. Deism was unpopular with the majority of his townsmen, and his persistence in its somewhat radical doctrines might detract from his influence. Moreover, he had watched it in operation in two of his companions and in himself and had concluded that, though it might be based in true principles, it was not useful. He expressed then, more or less conventionally, his belief in one God, who had made and who rules the universe, in immortality of the soul, in the punishment of evil and the rewarding of good. He advocated truth, sincerity, and integrity in dealing with men and thought the most acceptable service to God was one's doing good to men. Believing that a virtuous life has more chance of success than a nonvirtuous one, he made a chart of thirteen virtues, and, depending upon his own rationality and force of will, rather than on the

grace of God, which had been an absolute
with Edwards, he practiced each virtue
in turn for a week and accomplished four
rounds of the group in the fifty-two weeks
of a year. His was a mathematical attempt at virtuous living. If Franklin failed
at any time in some detail of his program,
he did not dress in a hair shirt to do pen-
ance, but recorded the lapse, if it were
serious enough, as an *erratum.* Neglect
of his fiancée, Deborah Read, while he
was in England, spending money that he
had been authorized to collect for an acquaintance, and flirting with the English
mistress of his friend James Ralph were
three such entries.

Though Franklin's pattern of living was
utilitarian, it was not basely utilitarian.
For Franklin was more than mere crafts-
man; he was an artist of the utilitarian;
that is, he had a vivid imagination, which
permitted him to envision that which the
hands might make for the more comfortable living of men. He could make lightning rods, for instance; but, while he was
at the task, he could think of the electric
currents that these rods would direct as
an organic part of a complex world which
might be simplified by man for his easier
living. Then, too, in making a thing useful, he generally started with the larger
objective of promoting order. One reads
of such an end between the lines of his
account of organizing the Post Office, and
the police, and words on a page. Orderli-
ness was one of his thirteen virtues, and
by his own testimony one of the most difficult of attainment.

The Franklin cultural tributary has
been more than a trickle in the current
of American and of world thought and
activity. I cannot assert that it has carried no obscuring sediment into the main
stream. Its temperature has proved so
attractive to modern man that he has re-
laxed in it perhaps more than he should.

Frugality in living is, I believe, the only
essential part of the Franklin pattern that
we have definitely forgot.

IV

The last of our trio, John Woolman,
was born in 1720. Like Franklin, he was
the son of parents who lived by the work
of their hands; like Edwards, he turned
to the ministry as a profession — the
Quaker ministry. He had many of the
characteristics of both his predecessors
all particularized by peculiar additions of
his own. He was a humanitarian, as was
Franklin, but from principle rather than
from expediency.

That as the Mind is moved [he wrote], by an
inward Principle , to love God as an invisible,
incomprehensible Being, by the same Principle it was moved to love him in all his
Manifestations in the visible World. That as
by his Breath the Flame of Life has kindled
in all sensible Creatures, to say that we love
God [as unseen] and at the same time exer-
cise cruelty toward the least Creature [mov-
ing by his life, or by life derived from Him],
is a contradiction in itself.

All men — rich and poor, black, white,
and red — were for him children of one
father and possessed of immortal souls.
No matter what their condition, they were
his brothers and sisters. So, they drew
from him a deep sympathy and a tender,
unobtrusive, and practical helpfulness.
When, after a visit into the South, he
knew the conditions under which sugar
was produced by slave labor, he left off
sugar; after he learned that the lives of
men and women employed in dyeing
cloth were shortened by occupational disease, he wore his clothing plain. He was
constantly watchful to avoid any luxury
the production of which could cause his
fellowman unnecessary labor. He made
his principle applicable even to the cabin

of a ship that carried him to England and so went steerage. ". . . the ideal which he sought," wrote one critic, "was a society in which no man should need to profit by the degradation of his fellowmen." One instance of his quiet methods of working among people sheds light on his character. About Christmas time of one year he was troubled by the drinking at the public-houses in his town, especially at one, where there was much disorder. "I believed it was incumbent on me," he wrote, "to go and speak to the Master of that House." But modesty, timidity, and humility restrained him. Franklin practiced humility consciously at times for social ends; Woolman was humble from knowing himself an insignificant creature dependent on God.

. . . with Prayers and Tears [he continues], I besought the Lord for his Assistance, who, in Loving-kindness gave me a resigned Heart: then, at a suitable opportunity, I went to the Public-House, and, seeing the Man amongst much Company, I went to him, and told him, I wanted to speak with him; so we went aside, and there, in the Fear of the Almighty, I expressed to him what rested on my Mind; which he took kindly, and afterwards showed more Regard to me than before.

In this same mild fashion, over wilderness paths from Massachusetts to South Carolina, he worked among the Quakers who held slaves for the liberation of these involuntary servants. In monthly, quarterly, and yearly meetings, his simple earnestness was gradually effective with the whole brotherhood, and in individual cases it frequently brought immediate emancipation of a slave. Concerning one trip into Virginia and North Carolina he writes:

I saw in these Southern Provinces so many Vices and Corruptions, increased by this Trade and this Way of Life, that it appeared to me as a Gloom over the Land; and though now many willingly run into it, yet, in future, the Consequence will be grievous to Posterity.

Franklin took an interest in the slavery question even to the point, I believe, of becoming a member of one of the earliest abolition groups, but his concern was never so personal, so close and heartfelt as Woolman's.

The same distinction holds between the two men in their relationships with the Indians. Franklin went once to Carlisle, Pennsylvania, to help draw a treaty with the Red Men, and, realizing that they were extremely apt to get drunk and be quarrelsome and disorderly, forbade the selling of liquor to them. But when they complained of the resolution, "we told them," he says, "that if they would continue sober during the treaty, we would give them plenty of rum when the business was over." Franklin describes the orgy that ensued after the rum was released, and then somewhat callously concludes:

. . . if it be the design of Providence to extirpate these savages in order to make room for cultivators of the earth, it seems not improbable that rum may be the appointed means. It has already annihilated all the tribes who formerly inhabited the sea-coast.

But Woolman was keenly aware of the suffering brought on the Indians by drink. He visualizes sympathetically the sequences of a scene such as had been merely picturesque to Franklin.

Their Skins and Furs [he says], gotten through much Fatigue and hard Travels in Hunting, with which they intended to buy Clothing, when they become intoxicated, they often sell at a low Rate for more Rum; and afterwards . . . they suffer for want of the necessaries of Life. . . . Where cunning People pass Counterfeits, and impose that on others which is good for nothing, it is considered as a Wickedness; but to sell that to People which we know does them Harm, and which often works their Ruin, for the Sake of Gain, manifests a hardened and corrupt Heart, and is an Evil, which demands the Care of all true Lovers of Virtue to suppress. . . .

During the period when Franklin, with fifty or sixty men, was constructing forts against the Indians, Woolman, whose Quaker views on warfare Franklin liked to ridicule, was with a single companion threading his way into the same region to labor quietly among the Indians, alongside a Moravian missionary, to show them the advantages of Christian living.

Woolman had the spiritual depth of Edwards, without the latter's high intelligence, and so in his expression he appears less studied, with a straightforward, frank simplicity that is earnest for but one end — transmission of the truth. He knew the dangers bred of fluency of speech and was careful to avoid them. On one occasion he spoke fluently, but realized immediately afterwards that he had exhibited himself rather than the truth.

As I was thus humbled and disciplined under the Cross [he wrote], my Understanding became more strengthened to distinguish the pure Spirit that inwardly moves upon the Heart, and taught me to wait in Silence, sometimes for many weeks together, till I felt that rise which prepares the creature to stand like a trumpet through which the Lord speaks to His flock.

Woolman had, also, much of the mystical insight and the devoutness that characterized Edwards. But he was more human, mingled more freely with men, understood and sympathized with their weaknesses.

Of these three eighteenth century Americans, two are almost forgotten. In comparison with their well-remembered contemporary, Franklin, do these two in their philosophies have any suggestions for us, equal to or surpassing his, of "what is most worth while in life and how to go about to achieve it"?

A. Whitney Griswold:
TWO PURITANS ON PROSPERITY

SINCE the German economist, Max Weber, first called serious attention to the relationship of Protestantism and capitalism, various scholars have become intrigued with the idea.[1] Some have taken issue with Weber on minor points, but most have accepted his general conclusions. R. H. Tawney, in particular, has elaborated the thesis, and integrated it with the history of the Reformation.[2]

[1] Weber's work first appeared in *Archiv fur Sozialwissenschaft und Sozialpolitik*, 1904–1905. It was published as a book in Germany in 1920 and afterwards translated into English and published as *The Protestant Ethic and the Spirit of Capitalism* (London, 1930).

[2] In *Religion and the Rise of Capitalism* (London, 1929). For an excellent review of both Weber

Reprinted by permission from A. W. Griswold, "Three Puritans on Prosperity," *The New England Quarterly*, Vol. VII (September, 1934), pp. 475–488. The original article was entitled "Three Puritans on Prosperity." The final section on the "Puritan," Timothy Dwight, has been eliminated in the interest of space. ED.

Ernst Troeltsch has shown its development in sectarian ethics.[3] Yet so far, no one has sought to demonstrate the forms in which this relationship has manifested itself in American history.

For three centuries, Americans have been taught to admire material success: the "frontier," perhaps, provided the economic basis for the lesson. The growing sense of nationalism, the democratic levelling of social barriers, immense natural resources have combined to make us a nation of "rugged individualists," intent upon getting rich. In addition, we have been harangued, severally and individually, on the virtue of making money by a race of success-prophets indigenous to our soil. It is with [two] early members of that race that this paper deals.

It is worth while, by way of orientation, to review, in brief, the essence of Weber's theory. Because no one has done this so concisely as Professor Morison, let us borrow from his *Builders of the Bay Colony:*

Max Weber, a German economist of the last century, propounded the interesting theory that Calvinism released the business man from the clutches of the priest, and sprinkled

holy water on economic success. According to him, John Calvin defended the taking of interest on loans, which the medieval church had condemned under the name of usury. Since God would not justify reprobates by prosperity, so the argument goes, the successful business man was probably one of God's elect; hence the Puritan sought success as evidence of his election to eternal bliss.

This is the theory to which Tawney, Troeltsch, and others have given added currency. Not so Mr. Morison. He rejects it on the grounds that "in none of the scores of funeral sermons which I have read, is it hinted 'Our departed friend was successful, so he must be in Heaven.'" Further, Mr. Morison proceeds to the conclusion of Professor Clive Day that "the economic ideas of the New England Puritans were medieval; and so far as their church had political power, it regulated rather than stimulated business enterprise."[4]

With the economic implications of the criticism of Messrs. Morison and Day, we are not specifically concerned. Yet their suggestion that "the economic ideas of the New England Puritans were medieval"[5] needs considerable qualification. In spite of the evidence offered by Mr. Day in support of this contention,[6] we can not overlook the failure of the collectivist experiment at Plymouth. It is incorrect to deny that at least the seeds of rugged individualism came over on the *Mayflower.* Later they grew so luxuriantly as to shut collectivism completely out of the Puritan sun. In partial proof

and Tawney, see Georgia Harkness, *John Calvin, The Man and His Ethics* (New York, 1931), 187–191. These, and other critics of Weber, have picked minor flaws in his argument, such as his over-simplification of Calvinism and his neglect of the social and economic origins of capitalism. They point out that before Luther and Calvin, Thomas Aquinas bestowed a rather negative sanction upon the virtue of thrift. But they uphold as sound Weber's main thesis, that since the Reformation, Protestantism has supplied both inspiration and ethical basis for the capitalist economy.

[3] In *The Social Teaching of the Christian Churches* (London, 1931). See also Preserved Smith, *The Age of the Reformation* (New York, 1920), and Reinhold Niebuhr, "Puritanism and Prosperity," in the *Atlantic Monthly*, cxxxvii, 721.

[4] S. E. Morison, *Builders of the Bay Colony* (Boston, 1930), 160.

[5] The words are Professor Morison's.

[6] Clive Hart Day, "Capitalistic and Socialistic Tendencies in the Puritan Colonies," *Annual Report of the American Historical Association . . . 1920* (Washington, 1925), 225–235.

of this we offer the sermons of our [two] Puritans.

Mr. Morison's criticism of the rational process suggested by Weber holds more water. Weber would have us believe that the New England farmer of Calvinist persuasion sought to make money not in order to secure the approval of God, but to prove to himself that God already had bestowed His approval, that he was already a member of the elect. The notion is over-subtle. Doubtless it has been entertained by wealthy merchants of the Back Bay and Salem; but, whether through inadvertence or shame, none seems to have committed it to writing. This does not justify the conclusion that Weber is entirely wrong. The fact is that God did "sprinkle holy water on economic success." Only He did it in a much more forthright manner, which the masses could understand, and which neither the Teutonic intellect of Herr Weber nor the sharp wit of Mr. Morison would have missed had they been citizens of that Puritan world. The [two] Puritans will speak for themselves. They are far from the old-world seats of learning. They address frontier audiences. They have no use for subtleties. They deal in plain truths for plain men.

II

Cotton Mather dealt most specifically with the relationship of business and religion in *Two Brief Discourses, one Directing a Christian in his General Calling; another Directing him in his Personal Calling*, a document of 1701 published in Boston the same year. Mather has become a much-quoted authority for the Weber thesis. Weber himself hastens over this document. It may profit us to turn its pages more leisurely. As its explicit title implies, the work deals with the rela-

tion of a man's business to his religion. There is a "calling" for each. The "general calling" is "to serve the Lord Jesus Christ," the "personal calling" "a certain Particular Employment by which his *Usefulness* in his neighborhood is distinguished."[7] Each is a matter of the utmost seriousness. A godly man must worship the Lord punctiliously. At the same time he should contract to do no business he "cannot comfortably venture to pray over." And he must have a business. Worshipping the Lord in prayer and hymn is not enough. Contemplation of the good means nothing without accomplishment of the good. A man must not only be pious; he must be useful.

Now it follows also, that a man must not only be useful but likewise successful. The Lord had made provision for that too. One should "be careful about the point: *What call from God have I to be in this place and at this work? Am I now where my Lord Jesus Christ would have me to be?*" After assuming this propitious attitude, he might safely trust in God "for the *Success* of all our *Business*, all the day long." But if he refused so to do, failure would be his lot, for "At no time of the Day, may we expect that our Business will succeed without *God's Blessing*."[8]

In Mather's congregation there must have been some logicians, especially among the business men. It was a comfort for them to hear their occupations sanctified. If they were to undertake no business they could not "comfortably venture to pray over," might they not calm uneasy consciences by praying harder? Might not the prayer draw up the business to its own level? We are not surprised to find Puritan merchants mention-

[7] Mather, *Two Brief Discourses*, 37.

[8] Mather, *Two Brief Discourses*, 22–23.

ing God prominently in their invoices — thanking Him for profit gained, or ascribing losses to His greater glory.[9] Neither are we at pains to discover one source of a typically American habit. Mention business to a business man, and he pulls a long face and assumes an air of mystery. This is not all pedantry. For business to Americans has been more than a struggle for existence, more than a career: it has been a "calling."

As for success in that calling, we need not depend on logic to be informed of what Mather thought of it. "A Christian, at his *Two Callings*," he elaborated, "is a man in a Boat, Rowing for Heaven; the House which our Heavenly Father hath intended for us. If he mind but one of his *Callings*, be it which it will, he pulls the *oar*, but on one side of the Boat, and will make but a poor dispatch to the Shoar of Eternal Blessedness." Let a man pray with might and main, he can not get to Heaven unless he attends well to his personal calling, "some *Settled Business*, wherein a Christian should for the most part spend most of his time [the words which follow are significant] and this, that so he may glorify God, by doing of *Good* for *others*, and getting of *Good* for *himself*."[10]

The meaning of these words is clear enough. We may have difficulty in reconciling the principles of "doing of *Good* for *others*," and "getting of *Good* for *himself*"; but that is the paradox which pervades the ethics of Protestantism. As we shall find in the pages which follow, it is sometimes hard to determine where the greater emphasis lies: whether upon a man's impersonal social usefulness, or on

his own individual economic success. Cotton Mather did not forget the welfare of society. He reminded his listeners that their occupations should not be anti-social, that they should "have a tendency to the Happiness of Mankind."[11] Yet we submit that Cotton Mather was thinking primarily as an individual, and that he was laying the true moral foundations for rugged American individualism.

The further he pursues his subject, the more specific become his rules of conduct.

Would a man *Rise* by his Business? I say, then let him *Rise* to his *Business*. It was foretold. Prov. 22. 29, *Seest thou a man Diligint* [sic] *in his Business? He shall stand before Kings;* He shall come to preferment. And it was instanced by him who foretold it; I Kings 11. 28. *Solomon, seeing that the young man was industrious, he made him a Ruler.* I tell you, with *Diligence* a man may do marvellous [sic] things. *Young* man, work hard while you are *Young;* You'l Reap the effects of it when you are *Old.* Yea, How can you Ordinarily enjoy any Rest at *Night*, if you have not been well at work in the *Day?* Let your *Business* engross the most of your time.[12] . . . Let every man have the *Discretion* to be well instructed in, and well acquainted with, all the mysteries of his *Occupation.* Be a master of your trade; count it a disgrace to be no workman.[13]

It may well have been that Mather himself thought of individual prosperity as an instrument of social welfare. But he presented it to his congregation first and foremost as both the temporal and spiritual reward for a life spent in industrious enterprise. Individuals should achieve salvation individually. Because industry tended to rally the Christian virtues

[9] William B. Weeden, *Economic and Social History of New England 1620–1789* (Boston and New York, 1890), I, 250.

[10] Mather, *Two Brief Discourses*, 38. The italics are Mather's.

[11] Mather, *Two Brief Discourses*, 49.

[12] Mather, *Two Brief Discourses*, 48.

[13] Mather, *Two Brief Discourses*, 53.

within a man, industry should be encouraged. Thus the material fruits of industry were blessed in the sight of God.

In Mather's system of the two complementary callings, God had the material success of individuals entirely at his disposal. Piety, therefore, was an instrument in achieving it. Practise the Christian virtues; kneel daily in prayer, and "all your *Business* will go on the better, all the day, for your being thus faithful to God."[14] The individual could be reassured by this. It meant that however he might lack in native ability, piety would repair the deficiency. He had Mather's word for it, for the latter said, "with the *Help of God* never fear, but your Hands will be sufficient for you."[15] To the democratic implications of this system we shall return directly. For the moment we may see in it another manifestation of God's concern for the individual prosperity of Puritan business men.

So far, it may be objected, we have judged Mather by only one sermon. Although of all his writings it is the one which deals most specifically with our subject, let us see if he afterwards changed his mind. Twenty years elapse, and he returns to the old theme in "The Vain Presumption of Living and Thriving in the World; which does too often possess and poison the *Children* of this *World.*"[16] A large congregation has assembled to hear him preach. The title gives a clue to the content. In 1720 too many people seem to have been finding economic success possible without piety. They have, as it were, been rowing themselves around in circles with the oar of "personal calling" and consequently are drifting away from the "Shoar of Eternal Blessedness." Mather pleads with them:

Acknowledge thy *Dependence* on the glorious God, for thy *Thriving* in the World. It is what we are minded of; Deut. VIII. 18. *Thou shalt remember the Lord thy God; for it is He that gives thee Power to get wealth.* Be sensible of this; *Riches* not always to them who are sharpest at inventing the most probable Methods of coming at it. Be sensible of this; The way to succeed in our Enterprizes, *O Lord, I know the way of man is not in himself!* Be sensible of this; In our *Occupation* we spread our *Nets;* but it is God who brings unto our *Nets* all that comes into them.[17]

One pictures a worldly congregation, some of which was no doubt thinking about other things than the sermon — of clever ways to outwit English customs-officers. Others, more serious, might have been wondering if God filled even smugglers' nets.

Mather has changed his emphasis but not his doctrine. God is still vitally interested in man's economic lot. He still desires that to be successful. Moreover, according to the great divine, God had vouchsafed success to the poorest mortals, to men of the humblest parts. For wealth was "not always to them who are sharpest at inventing the most probable methods of coming at it." The social ethics embodied in Mather's preaching were reflected in the exigencies of frontier life — or did the ethics reflect the frontier? It is often asserted that religion generally sanctions the customs of society. What of the Puritanism of Cotton Mather? The most eminent spiritual leader of the Puritans for half a century, he held up to them an ideal of success to be achieved for the glory of God. Conditions on the frontier made collectivism difficult: at Plymouth

14 Mather, *Two Brief Discourses,* 67.

15 Mather, *Two Brief Discourses,* 69.

16 Cotton Mather, *Sober Sentiments,* funeral sermon, *Produced by the Premature and Much-lamented Death of Mr. Joshua Lamb* (Boston, 1722).

17 Mather, *Sober Sentiments,* 25.

it was tried and abandoned. Servants were lured away by the opportunity to acquire farms of their own for nothing. Wages, in several colonies, became so exorbitant as to necessitate statutory limits. Most obvious of all, one had to work in the wilderness, or die. Conditions demanded precisely the same moral qualities of industry, perseverance, sobriety, thrift, and prudence, as did Cotton Mather. They stressed, likewise, individual enterprise. Indeed, we might suppose that the frontier would have created a system of social ethics closely resembling Mather's if America had never heard of Luther and Calvin, were it not for one phrase which lingers: Wealth "not always to them who are sharpest at inventing the most probable methods of coming at it." This was the perfervid hope which the Puritanism of Cotton Mather held out to the common man. It meant, in humble ken, that God had made provision for all men to succeed.

As worldliness crept into the Puritan religion, occasioning the desperate effort of Jonathan Edwards to revive the fire and brimstone of primitive Calvinism, the social ethics preached by Mather did not die. American Protestants became divided into hostile sects: Methodists, Baptists, Unitarians. Some called themselves Deists. But as a general rule, their business remained a vital part of their religion, a calling. God continued to fill the nets of individual enterprise. Call it rationalization, hypocrisy, inspiration, or what you will, Puritans clung to the doctrine that God would point the way to individual prosperity, and would be pleased at its achievement.

Cotton Mather did not invent this doctrine: he merely gave it expression. His utterances are of interest to us not so much for the persuasive influence they may have had upon his contemporaries,

as because they represent the mind of orthodox Puritanism two centuries ago. They indicate that thinking men were casting about in their minds for a moral sanction for money-making, and that they found that sanction in the ethical system originally propounded by Martin Luther and John Calvin. Thus, in a sense, Cotton Mather deserves recognition as one of the first to teach American business men to serve God by making money.

III

One day in 1724 Cotton Mather received a young caller at his home in Boston. It was a sober youth of eighteen years who presented himself. Benjamin Franklin had returned from Philadelphia for a brief visit to his native town, and had stopped to pay his respects to the great Puritan, whom he much admired. Franklin's later account of the visit indicates that it made some impression on him. Mather

. . . received me in his library [he wrote] and on my taking leave showed me a shorter way out of the house, through a narrow passage, which was crossed by a beam overhead. We were talking as I withdrew, he accompanying me behind, and I turning partly towards him, when he said hastily, *"Stoop, stoop!"* I did not understand him till I felt my head hit against the beam. He was a man that never missed any occasion of giving instruction, and upon this he said to me: *"You are young, and have the world before you;* STOOP *as you go through it, and you will miss many hard thumps."* This advice, thus beat into my head, has frequently been of use to me, and I often think of it when I see pride mortified and misfortunes brought upon people by carrying their heads too high.[18]

Was this all that Mather had to offer his

[18] Benjamin Franklin, *Complete Works* (New York, 1887), VIII, 484–485.

visitor; or was there a real spiritual bond between the two?

The God in which Franklin consistently professed belief was far more genial than Cotton Mather's stern Jehovah. Out of a vast "Chorus of Worlds" He was merely "that particular Wise and good God, who is the author and owner of our System."[19] His greatest gift to man was reason, by which man might discover his true function in the scheme of things. So glaring are the inconsistencies in Franklin's life that we take whatever he said with many grains of salt. We should not, for example, attach too much importance to the "Articles of Faith and Acts of Religion" which he drew up, with solemn precocity at the age of twenty-two. His life proclaims him too palpable a *citoyen du monde* to warrant much attention to his theology. Yet by virtue of this fact, it is all the more intriguing that he should have subscribed to a system of ethics identical to Cotton Mather's. In his life Franklin was a Deist, if not an out-and-out agnostic; in his writings, he was the soul of Puritanism. Why was this?

To be sure, Franklin had been born a Puritan in Puritan society. In childhood he heard his father admonish him over and over again on the inestimable value of all the Puritan virtues. But neither heredity nor environment can wholly account for Dr. Franklin. Was there some spiritual kinship, then, some intellectual contact with Puritan philosophers? Franklin himself says there was. The books which he precociously read numbered among them Pilgrim's Progress, Plutarch, and the works of Daniel Defoe. But it was from none of these that the spark of Franklin's Puritanism flashed. If we are to take him at his word, we must consider rather a small volume entitled *Essays to*

Do Good by the Reverend Cotton Mather. This, he says in the *Autobiography*, "perhaps gave me such a turn of thinking that had an influence on some of the principle future events of my life."[20] And in 1784, from the terminus of his great career, he wrote Cotton Mather's son renewing the acknowledgment. The *Essays* had given him "such a turn of thinking, as to have an influence on my conduct through life, for I have always set a greater value on the character of a *doer of good,* than on any other kind of reputation; and if I have been, as you seem to think, a useful citizen, the public owes the advantage of it to that book."[21]

Before rejecting Franklin's compliments as insincere, let us see what Mather had to say to him. Let us pause, for a moment, over the strange intellectual kinship of the author of *The Wonders of the Invisible World,* and the man who "discovered" electricity. The central theme of the *Essays to Do Good* is that of the sermons: personal salvation achieved through good works. The two callings receive lengthy treatment; and there is a categorical exposition of methods of doing good. Ministers, school teachers, lawyers, physicians all have their specific functions. But the greatest opportunity awaits persons of wealth. To them Mather has something special to say:

Sirs, you cannot but acknowledge that it is the sovereign God who has bestowed upon you the riches which distinguish you. A devil himself, when he saw a rich man, could not but make this acknowledgment to the God of heaven: "Thou hast blessed the work of his hands, and his substance is increased in the land."[22]

[19] Franklin, *Works,* I, 308.

[20] Franklin, *Works,* I, 44: this was written in 1771.

[21] Franklin, *Works,* VIII, 484.

[22] Mather, *Essays to Do Good:* American Tract Society (Boston, 1710), 86–87.

But the divine esteem enjoyed by the man of property does not diminish his obligations to society. The Lord has made him His "steward." He has charged him with a sacred trust, charity. Moreover, God in His infinite wisdom has made charity an attractive sacrifice, for if we are to believe Cotton Mather, the charitable

... very frequently ... have been rewarded with remarkable success in their affairs, and increase of their property; and even in this world have seen the fulfillment of those promises: "Cast thy bread upon the waters" — thy grain into the moist ground — "and thou shalt find it after many days." "Honor the Lord with thy substance; so shall thy barns be filled with plenty." History has given us many delightful examples of those who have had their *decimations* followed and rewarded by a surprising prosperity of their affairs. Obscure mechanics and husbandmen have risen to estates, of which once they had not the most distant expectation.[23]

So spoke the Reverend Cotton Mather to young Ben Franklin. His words are at once corroborative and prophetic. They are further evidence of his belief in the piety of individual prosperity, and they whisper of the future when thousands of "obscure mechanics and husbandmen" would rise (as millions would aspire) "to estates of which they had not the most distant expectation."

It would be interesting to lay the texts of Mather's *Essays* and Franklin's *Autobiography* side by side, so much is the former reflected in the latter. The purpose in recording his own rise "from the poverty and obscurity in which I was born and bred, to a state of affluence and some degree of reputation in the world,"[24] Franklin declares, is to allow others to profit by his example. He himself thought

it "fit to be imitated" and therefore he would write a book about it. But first he desired "with all humility to acknowledge that I owe the mentioned happiness of my past life to [God's] kind providence, which led me to the means I used and gave them success."[25] How like a Puritan to attribute to the Lord "a state of affluence and some degree of reputation in the world." The *Autobiography* is filled with similar professions of humility and piety. To the uncritical reader, the sermon it preached must have seemed even more convincing than Mather's, for it had received from its author the pragmatic sanction of successful practice. So he declared, at any rate. He had found it helpful as a young printer's apprentice to draw up a chart of the virtues necessary for complete moral perfection, and then to score himself daily on progress made — or not made. Mather himself could not have improved the list. It included temperance, silence, order, resolution, frugality, industry, sincerity, justice, moderation, cleanliness, tranquillity, chastity, and humility. Of these, industry was most important. "Lose no time," he said to himself, "be always employed in something useful; cut off all unnecessary actions."[26]

But it is *Poor Richard* who sings the loudest praise of industry. Luck, says he, is of no account. Americans need only work hard and never trouble themselves about luck, for "*Diligence is the Mother of good luck,* and *God gives all things to industry.*" *Poor Richard* likewise knows all about the calling: "*He that hath a trade hath an estate, and he that hath a calling hath an office of profit and honor.*"[27] In fact the way to wealth was,

[23] Mather, *Essays to Do Good,* 89–90.
[24] Franklin, *Works,* I, 29.
[25] Franklin, *Works,* I, 30–31.
[26] Franklin, *Works,* I, 176.
[27] Franklin, *Works,* I, 444.

in his own words, "as plain as the way to market" to Benjamin Franklin.

It depends chiefly on two words, *industry* and *frugality* — that is, waste neither *time* nor *money*, but make the best use of both. Without industry and frugality nothing will do, and with them everything. He that gets all he can and saves all he can . . . will certainly become rich, if that Being who governs the world, to whom all should look for a blessing on their honest endeavors, doth not, in his wise providence, otherwise determine.[28]

Did Franklin learn all this from Cotton Mather? It is authentic Puritanism. Mather had, at times, stooped low enough to commend charity as a profitable business venture. Franklin certainly knew Mather and read his works. Yet the man who paraphrased classic aphorisms for simple Americans feared no Puritan God. The thunderbolt which was the angry voice of Jehovah to Mather trickled harmlessly off a wet kite-string into Franklin's Leyden jar. *Poor Richard's* wisdom is savory with business acumen. Whence, therefore, the piety? Was it an afterthought?

It makes little difference where Franklin got his Puritanism. Very likely Mather made substantial contributions. Yet the piety, in all probability, was no afterthought. It was put there with deliberate intent. Let us not forget that Benjamin Franklin was a journalist and publisher by trade. *Poor Richard's Almanac*, like

most of his other publications, was distinctly a money-making venture. Its shrewd author knew his trade; and what was more, he knew his public. Any publisher knows that catering to a public's taste is profitable, and that is precisely what Franklin did. He understood Puritanism well enough to realize that it offered assurances of material prosperity to all who followed its code of morals. Piety was inexpensive, and so although he himself was worlds apart from orthodoxy, he preached Puritan ethics as good as Mather's. From an unmoral point of view he perceived that the Puritan virtues had immense utilitarian value. And, skeptic though he was, he doubtless thought it wise to be on the safe side, to propitiate whatever God there might be. However that may be, he knew his public would think so.

The popularity of his writings bears witness to Franklin's shrewdness. The *Autobiography* became a famous American success story. Let its author be accused of hypocrisy in affecting the moral austerity of Puritanism. His public must have been delighted to find that he, a scientist, a patriot, a man who had in actuality risen to "a state of affluence and some degree of reputation in the world" endorsed the same democratic virtues as their ministers. It must have relieved them to have such a man turn thumbs down on chance, as it rejoiced them to hear him re-affirm the sanctity of individual prosperity. Benjamin Franklin not only commended prosperity; he dramatized it. . . .

[28] Franklin, *Works*, II, 120–121.

Gladys Meyer:

THE URBAN PATTERN OF SUCCESS

SOME writers have stressed Franklin's sane estimate of the value of money and his essential public spiritedness in his early retirement from business. A more searching interpretation would suggest that Franklin continued to increase his wealth by speculation and investment even without active management of his business. In his business itself, his experiments with magazines and the foreign language press showed that he had reached the limits of possible expansion in the kinds of product he could introduce. With increased wealth alone, furthermore, he most probably could not have elevated himself further in the social scale, for his origin was for all social purposes unknown, he had not known the proprietor and his circle, and neither he nor his wife had the taste or the connections to conduct the social life of the inner circle.

His retirement must be interpreted in terms, as indeed he stated himself, of needing more time, first to experiment and second for the conduct of political life which was the natural terrain for his manipulating genius.

Franklin clearly developed certain techniques for personal social advancement. Good repute, the strength of association, the threat of adverse publicity, the use of patronage, the accumulation of wealth, the interest in civic improvement, interplayed continually to promote his rise. It is interesting as a preface to understanding his values to ask at what personal cost this technique was perfected.

To raise the question of the relation between Franklin's public and private personality, and of the character and integrity of his procedure, is difficult because Franklin was discreet and always aware of the public to whom he spoke, if and when he revealed himself at all. His biography, seemingly so candid, is a masterpiece of discretion. He had no intimate friend, letters to whom might give any direct clue to his inner spirit. "Let all men know thee, but no man know thee thoroughly," advised Poor Richard.

It is apparent that as a young man the gap between Franklin's behavior and the demands of custom for good character were wide. The curious, observant, adventurous young apprentice in Boston and in London had little concern for the world's opinion of him. Slowly he began to be aware of the force of social pressure. His brother was imprisoned for speaking boldly. In London the printers broke up his forms when he would not observe their customs. His casualness in lending money brought him privation. It became apparent that if he were to survive he would have to modify his unpatterned behavior.

He modified quickly in externals. He set about to give the appearance of hard work, of simplicity and content, and to speak, through his paper and his almanack, moral precepts for the general public. Inside Franklin there was a picture of the gentleman of wealth and leisure. If wealthy Franklin said through Poor Richard "Content makes poor men rich,"

From Gladys Meyer, *Free Trade in Ideas* (New York: King's Crown Press, 1941), pp. 70–71, 72–75, 86–88, with permission of the publisher.

struggling Franklin let Poor Richard say at an earlier date (1736) "He that can have patience can have what he will." His inner spirit was ambitious and aggressive, but he created a front which was soft spoken.

The objections and reluctances I met with in soliciting the subscriptions, [he writes in the Autobiography,] made me soon feel the impropriety of presenting oneself as the proposer of any useful project, that might be supposed to raise one's reputation in the smallest degree above that of one's neighbors, when one has need of their assistance to accomplish that project. I therefore put myself as much as I could out of sight, and stated it was a scheme of *a number of friends* who had requested me to go about and propose it. [author's italics]

"Let thy discontents be secrets" advises Poor Richard repeatedly.

In order to resolve the tensions created by the division of Franklin's public and private character he worked out for himself a table of precepts for virtuous behavior, and systematically endeavored to make their observance become habit. . . . [The author here lists Franklin's table of moral precepts.]

This famous and curious list of virtues Franklin pursued with regular plan, devoting a week to each at a time, and keeping a chart on which he noted all failures. The spirit of rational planning dominated him in his attempt to harness his creative energies to customary channels. Franklin as an old man said that he had mastered them all tolerably well except order. Here his unfettered spirit kept breaking through.

It broke through in other ways, too. There are clear discrepancies between his public personality in the Autobiography, and his private letters. One illustration will suffice.

Having been sometime employed by the postmaster general of America, [he writes in the account of his life,] as his comptroller in regulating several offices, and bringing officers to account, I was upon his death in 1753, appointed jointly with Mr. William Hunter to succeed him.

Compare this with his letter to Collinson in May 1751.

I have not heretofore made much Scruple of giving you Trouble when the Publick Good was to be promoted by it, but 't is with great Reluctance that I think of asking you to interest yourself in my private Concerns, as I know you have so little Time to spare. The Place is in the disposal of the Postmasters General of Britain with some of whom or with their Friends you may possibly have Acquaintance. . . . I am quite a stranger in the Manner of Managing these Applications so can offer no particular instructions. I enclose a Copy of the Commission of a former Deputy Post Master General which may be of some Use. . . . The Place has commonly been reputed worth about £150 a Year, but would otherways be very suitable to me, particularly as it would enable me to execute a Scheme long since formed of which I send you enclosed a Copy, and which I hope would soon produce something agreeable to you and All Lovers of Useful Knowledge, for I now have a large Acquaintance among ingenious Men in America. [The project is the American Philosophical Society.] I need not tell you that Philadelphia being the Center of the Continent Colonies and having constant Communication with the West India islands is by much a fitter Place for the Situation of a General Post Office than Virginia, and that it would be some Reputation to our Province to have it established here. I would only add that as I have respect for Mr. Benger I should be glad if the Application were so managed as not give him any Offense if he should recover. . . . [This was two years before Benger's death] p.s. I have heard that £200 was given for this Office by Mr. Benger and the same by his Predecessor.

I know not whose Perquisite it was. But lest that should not be sufficient and there may be some contingent Fees and Charges, Mr. Allen has ordered £ 300. However, the less it costs the better, as 't is for Life only which is very uncertain Tenure.

The autobiographical account is the brief sketch of a public servant rewarded for faithfulness. Yet the reward was not chance. "Diligence is the mother of good luck," says Poor Richard, and diligence in promoting his interests is apparent in Franklin's approach to Collinson. One can observe how Franklin rewards Collinson for the service by pointing out that the office will be of use in furthering the scientific interests which they have in common. If Franklin had scruples in using his scientific friendship to further his personal ambition, he overcame them. "Bargaining has neither friends nor relations," says Poor Richard.

The patron saint of industry and frugality, Franklin nevertheless enjoyed conspicuous display, within limits. He liked to wear a uniform. He kept a negro page for his son, and had household slaves which his autobiography never mentions. And his use of Quaker dress when he was presented to the King of France is an inverted use of the same mode of creating distinction.

An indication of Franklin's front is the manner in which he met defeat. In the election of 1764, after his defeat in the Assembly he went home and went to bed. "Mr. Franklin died like a philosopher" says a contemporary. Whatever he felt he concealed. When he was tried before the Privy Council "he stood," says an eye witness, if Parton's account is correct, "conspicuously erect, without the smallest movement of any part of his body. The muscles of his face had been previously composed so as to afford a placid, tranquil expression of countenance, and

he did not suffer the slightest alteration of it to appear." When his severest blow came and his son turned Loyalist he ceased to speak to him. In each case Franklin won confidence and respect by his composure.

What did Franklin imagine himself to be? His earliest portrait, which he commissioned on his retirement from business, shows a rather pompous man, sober and self respecting. The portrait which he commissioned for his family while he was in England shows the influence of his scholarly achievements. Here we have a Georgian gentleman in his study. In the first portrait he is wearing somber dress, showing the prudent and modest public figure he wished to create in the home city. In the English portrait he saw himself a scientist, for this was the only sphere in which he could compete in England. He presented this one to the State of Pennsylvania on his death. The French portraits show a curious difference. Greuze has drawn a rather tired old man, disillusioned, perhaps even tender. Duplessis shows a calculating shrewd countenance and cold eyes. Neither of these portraits were favorites of Franklin. He liked ones which gave him a bright, sprightly expression, like the bust of Houdon.

Whom did he love and whom did he trust? Can this give us a key to his personality? "Distrust and Caution are the parents of Security," says the first Almanack. Politically he trusted no one, though he respected a service. He never betrayed, for example, who procured the Hutchinson letters for him. But as he rose in position he saw his friendships waver. William Allen dropped away after the military display. Galloway, with whom he left the management of his affairs while he was in England, went over to the Loyalists at the outbreak of the Revolution. The circumstances of war severed him from close connection with the circle he had enjoyed in England. His long residence abroad deprived him of intimate friends at home. His wife was always the recipient of his affectionate attention, but he seldom confided in her. He hardly knew his daughter until he was very old and she a matron. His son and his grandsons were the ones he leaned on most. But he never understood them as persons. He had educated William to be a gentleman, brought him to England for ten impressionable years of young manhood, got him an appointment as Royal Governor of New Jersey, saw him marry the daughter of a West India planter, and then wondered why he turned Loyalist. He always over-estimated the talents of his grandson, Temple, whom he kept constantly with him. (Temple was the illegitimate son of William Franklin.) He tried to marry Temple into the French court circle, but without success. "He that will win the race runs by himself" wrote Franklin in 1747.

Looking at Franklin's Philadelphia career, and the pattern of action which it established, patience, long term investment, judgment, division of risk, emerge as the clear attributes of personal as well as economic success. The importance of good will, with the accompanying conformity of manners, was as clear to Franklin as to those making up the assets for a corporation balance sheet. Adaptability in the face of change and its accompanying versatility of interest are important if one is to move to more widely extended spheres of action in a competitive society.

Franklin's approach to human relationships, as may be seen when his practise is analyzed, was that of the true entrepreneur: resources were to be organized, and this was his great talent. A fair bargain was to be struck. Thus he sought and re-

turned favors, returning in flattery when he could not in kind. When circumstances forced a change of relationships he kept silent. He played his human relationships as one hedges on the market, adapting quickly to changes and not raising the question of ultimate loyalties. For this reason, although his repute grew, his personal security lessened. His last stronghold was the family, and he was true to his pattern in packing the post offices with his relatives. Where family loyalty failed he became an isolated human being in a depersonalized world.

Franklin, experimental, enquiring, discreetly bold, rationalistic, self disciplined, was the personal embodiment of the conditions of capitalistic success. And in his combination of individual shrewdness and wide tolerance he was the quintessence of eighteenth century liberalism. He not only had in himself those characteristics which were in eminent harmony with the conditions of capitalist development, but he was in his lifetime recognized as the symbol of the new era. He appeared at the exact right moment in history to express the international figure of the successfully emergent merchant entrepreneur. . . .

Before raising the question of the enduring value of Franklin's liberalism, what in summary, are the characteristics of Franklin's career that serve as background for this "ideal type" of American liberal?

First and foremost he was an individual who rose in the social scale more spectacularly than almost any other before him. The environment in which he rose was urban. It had not the isolation of a rural community, nor the simpleness of rural social structure. It was, however, not metropolitan, but was sufficiently small to permit an interlocking network of face to face groups. Without this wide and yet diversified group support Franklin could not have achieved so remarkable a degree of social influence. The many separate groups exerting social pressure, offered the individual career the advantage of division of risk in case of major or minor defeats.

Franklin by his single individual shift of status could not have become the mouthpiece of eighteenth century American liberalism. He could only become so because the history of the western world was seeing the successful establishment of the domination of the merchant entrepreneurs. The collective ascent of a group in Philadelphia gave him his clearly defined role, and it assumed magnitude because Philadelphia was repeating in two generations what Europe had struggled with for two centuries.

No world position could have been more favorable for the emergence of the spokesman of the economic liberal tradition in its full social interrelationships. Franklin was ahead of his locality through his experience in London, his knowledge of other colonies, and through his faithful and detailed reading of the foreign press. And his career was crowned and his reputation completed by long residence in the two significant capitals of eighteenth century Europe.

Franklin had grown up in the most highly articulate society in America — Boston. He had therefore, the concepts and the speech to give voice to popular thought of the colonial people, urban and rural, who were his subscribers.

America, before 1750, at the time of Franklin's Philadelphia residence, furthermore was one place in the world where rural-urban tension was not yet acute. The freeholders of Pennsylvania, producing for export, except at the outskirts on the frontier, understood risk and investment as well as the ship owner.

They did not have centuries of village life behind them.

Franklin was a publisher. Everywhere in the world in the eighteenth century liberalism was carried by publishers. They became the handmaids of the insurgent class because this class, lacking privilege, needed to claim its rights, and the press became the chief channel for making its claims.

Every country saw the merchants, Jews, and Freemasons as the patrons of liberalism in salon, school, press or public discussion. Franklin had established social relationships with all of these.

Not only did Franklin lay such a heavy imprint on the American liberal tradition because he was the great American success story, but because he caught and restated through his mouthpiece, Poor Richard, the "Volksgeist," so that his precepts became part of traditional American mores.

This career produced a man whose aim in life was always that of bearing a specific relationship to people. In order to gain this relationship, and the extension of personality it allowed, he was willing to plan, to wait, to invest, to undergo great disciplinary effort. This gave him an intellectual focus on method, which in behavior terms became an emphasis on habit — a way of systematizing behavior and making it more efficient. His ends were concrete and relative, and he acted always as the astute opportunist.

Out of his experience Franklin created a pattern for later liberals who have kept hoping for modification of the status quo, who rely for social control on the free association of individuals who come together for shorter or longer periods of time on the basis of their interests, who are divorced from a dogmatic program, who campaign for tolerance that their own shifting activities may not be limited.

Franklin furthermore may be called a liberal because he advocated those principles of public action which have historically been the terms of the liberal campaign, freedom of speech, of the press, and that relation of liberty and discretion which seeks to confine change to orderly process within the existing social framework.

Is the belief that such discretionary change is possible a characteristic of a member of a rising group which becomes successfully integrated into the social structure, whose frustrations are not acute and whose economic life is not in jeopardy? Is it a corollary, then, of an expanding economy, and its popular acceptance dependent on a widespread hope for economic improvement?

As we have seen from Franklin's activities, liberalism may flourish in a society replete with face to face associations, each somewhat different in the details of purpose and method, with overlapping membership, each empirical in their approach to public policy. Can those conditions continue in an increasingly complex social and economic structure?

Charles Angoff: BENJAMIN FRANKLIN

... [FRANKLIN] was the first great fixer of American political history, and also, if John Adams is to be believed, its first great trimmer. He made friends of the English, he made friends of the French, he made friends of the Germans, he made friends of the Federalists, he made friends of the Republicans, and when he died the whole civilized world mourned him. Just where he stood on any one of the fundamental issues is still something of a mystery. He trusted the people, and he didn't trust them. He claimed to be a deist, but he contributed to all the churches in his neighborhood, and believed in the transmigration of souls. All his life long he preached a copy-book morality, but he himself was extremely careless in his personal affairs. He spent money lavishly, ate so much that he suffered from gout for years and years, and when he was married at the age of twenty-four brought to his wife, as a wedding present, an illegitimate son.

He wrote a great deal, but it was chiefly to make money, or to forget the pain of his gout. He knew his public well. He made a fortune as a newspaper and a magazine editor, and his "Poor Richard's Almanac" was an immediate success: it sold 10,000 copies within the first three months of publication. He did not produce one truly great work of the imagination, and his general style was surely not above the ordinary, but his work achieved an amazing popularity.

All this was probably a colossal misfortune to the United States, for, despite his good fellowship and occasional good sense, Franklin represented the least praiseworthy qualities of the inhabitants of the New World: miserliness, fanatical practicality, and lack of interest in what are usually known as spiritual things. Babbittry was not a new thing in America, but he made a religion of it, and by his tremendous success with it he grafted it upon the American people so securely

From Charles Angoff, *A Literary History of the American People* (New York: Alfred A. Knopf, 1931), pp. 295–310. Use by permission of the author.

that the national genius is still suffering from it. He extolled the virtues of honesty, industry, chastity, cleanliness, and temperance — all excellent things. But it never occurred to him that with these alone life is not worth a fool's second thought. Philosophy, poetry, and the arts spring from different sources. . . .

[Here follows a summary of Franklin's career which can be reconstructed from the chronology at the beginning of this volume.]

One American critic has said, "Intellectually there are few men who are Franklin's peers in all the ages and nations." This opinion must be put down as an amiable exaggeration. Franklin had an excellent mind, but surely he was not a philosopher. Abstract ideas, save those of the corner grocery store, somehow irked him. He was not an original thinker, but he was one of the best eclectic thinkers who ever lived. He lived in an age of rationalism, and few other men of that time were so imbued with the ideas then afloat. The current French philosophy was in large part precisely to his taste. "In their youth, Voltaire and Franklin had both drunk at the same spring: the English radicalism of Gordon, Collins, and Shaftesbury. But Voltaire had developed it into a witty, dry and sharp-tongued philosophy, while Franklin had expanded it with good fellowship and sentimentality."

This good fellowship of his explains his strange brand of deism. He was not a believer, but there were many reservations to his unbelief. In Paris he refused to have any priests around him, and this caused much surprise in a land where every diplomat had his private chaplain. He told everybody that he could say his prayers himself. "He considered the Church of Rome to be like raw sugar, the American churches like refined sugar, for they were less influenced by hierarchical systems of mysticism. He saw a certain advantage in the multiplicity of churches in the world, as that made for competition and competition made for trade, but he didn't think churches were of any importance in Heaven." He spoke of miracles with levity, but he had some belief in Pythagoreanism. In other words, he was pretty much confused about the whole business. His main contribution to the religious question was little more than a good-natured tolerance influenced largely by his shrewd business sense. Nobody but Franklin could have reconciled deism with the practice of contributing money to all the denominations in Philadelphia.

On the few occasions when he tried to be philosophical about religion he made a sorry spectacle, as in the following celebrated letter to Dr. Ezra Stiles, president of Yale. The letter is dated March 9, 1790 — a little more than a month before Franklin's death.

You desire to know something of my Religion. It is the first time that I have been questioned upon it. But I do not take your curiosity amiss, & shall endeavor in a few words to gratify it. Here is my Creed. I believe in one God, Creator of the Universe: That he governs the World by his Providence. That he ought to be worshipped. That the most acceptable service we can render to him, is doing good to his other Children. That the Soul of Man is immortal, and will be treated with Justice in another Life, respect^g its Conduct in this. These I take to be the fundamental Principles of all sound Religion, and I regard them as you do, in whatever Sect I meet with them. As to *Jesus of Nazareth*, my Opinion of whom you particularly desire, I think the *System of Morals & his Religion as he left them to us, the best the World ever saw*; but I apprehend it has received various corrupting changes; and I have, with most of the present Dissenters in Engld, some Doubts as to his Divinity: tho' it is a question I do not dogmatize upon, hav^g never studied it,   think it needless to busy myself with it now, when I expect soon an Opport^y of know^g the Truth with less Trouble. I see no harm however in its being believed, if that Belief has the good Consequence, as probably it has, of mak^g his Doctrines more respected   better observed, esp^y as I do not perceive that the Supreme [Being] takes it amiss, by distinguish^g the Believers, in his Gov^t of the World, with any particular Marks of his Displeasure. I shall only add respect^g myself, that hav^g experienced the Goodness of that Being in conducting me prosperously thro' a long Life, I have no doubt of its Continuance in the next, tho' without the smallest Conceit of meriting such Goodness.

Try to imagine Thomas Paine dismissing God and the churches in so flippant a way!

Franklin's most popular work was, and still is, his "Autobiography." It was the longest of his writings, and the one he did most carelessly. He wrote it whenever he felt like it, and apparently cared very little if it was ever published. The greater part of it he composed while he was in England as agent for the United Colonies. Parts of it were printed in France between 1791 and 1798, but the complete "Autobiography" did not appear till 1868 under the editorship of John Bigelow, who copied it from the original MS., which he obtained in France.

John Bach McMaster, the historian, has called the book the greatest biographical work of any kind ever written in America, and has compared it to Defoe's "Robinson Crusoe" in literary merit. The book is very simply written, and is quite readable. But it is lacking in almost everything else necessary to a really great work of *belles lettres*: grace of expression, charm of personality, and intellectual flight. The essential commonplaceness of the man is in every line of it. He was incapable of

dreaming, of doubting, of being mystified. The only mysteries he understood were those that lent themselves easily to experimentation. The mysteries of poetry, of philosophy, and even of religion were beyond him. Doing good, making money, and gaining the approbation of one's fellows were the only things that occupied him when addressing the public. Witness his "Scheme for Aiming at Moral Perfection": [Here follows Franklin's account of his plan for arriving at moral perfection and his table of moral precepts.]

Not a word about nobility, not a word about honor, not a word about grandeur of soul, not a word about charity of mind! Carlyle called Franklin the father of all the Yankees. That was a libel against the tribe, for the Yankees have produced Thoreau, Hawthorne, and Emily Dickinson. It would be more accurate to call Franklin the father of all the Kiwanians.

Franklin began his "Poor Richard's Almanac" in December, 1732. It was an imitation of the English "Poor Robin's Almanac.". . .

Bigelow thinks that "Poor Richard" contains "some of the best fun as well as the wisest counsel that ever emanated from Franklin's pen." That is quite true, but absolutely considered the wisdom is of a low order. It points downward. True enough, it was addressed to the common man, but one does not always have to be a vulgarian when talking to the man in the street. Consider Jesus and Socrates and Confucius and Lao-tze. Consider Montaigne. Consider even Krylov. . . . [The author here supplies representative epigrams from "Poor Richard."]

Of "The Bagatelles," which Franklin wrote while he was in France, little more can be said than for "Poor Richard." Even after more than ten years of Parisian salon life he could not forget his twopenny philosophy. . . .

Franklin perpetrated one more piece of literature that has somehow escaped the literary historians, but that surely deserves mention. That was his proposed new version of the Bible. Like the immortal authors of the Bay Psalm Book he did not like the King James version. He said:

It is now more than one hundred and seventy years since the translation of our common English Bible. The language in that time is much changed, and the style being obsolete, and thence less agreeable, is perhaps one reason why the reading of that excellent book is of late so much neglected. I have therefore thought it well to procure a new version in which, preserving the sense, the turn of phrase and manner of expression should be modern. I do not pretend to have the necessary abilities for such a work myself; I throw out the hint for the consideration of the learned.

The following was his idea of how the first chapter of Job should read:

Verse 6. *King James version.* Now there was a day when the sons of God came to present themselves before the Lord, and Satan came also amongst them.

Verse 6. *New version by Franklin.* And it being *levee* day in heaven, all God's nobility came to court, to present themselves before him; and Satan also appeared in the circle, as one of the ministry.

Verse 7. *King James version.* And the Lord said unto Satan: Whence comest thou? Then Satan answered the Lord, and said: From going to and fro in the earth, and from walking up and down in it.

Verse 7. *New version by Franklin.* And God said to Satan: you have been some time absent; where were you? And Satan answered: I have been at my country-seat, and in different places visiting my friends.

Verse 8. *King James version.* And the Lord said unto Satan: Hast thou considered my servant Job, that there is none like him in the earth, a perfect and an upright man, one that feareth God, and escheweth evil?

Verse 8. *New version by Franklin.* And God said: Well, what do you think of Lord Job? You see he is my best friend, a perfectly honest man, full of respect for me, and avoiding everything that might offend me.

Verse 9. *King James version.* Then Satan answered the Lord, and said: Doth Job fear God for naught?

Verse 9. *New version by Franklin.* And Satan answered: Does your Majesty imagine that his good conduct is the effect of mere personal attachment and affection?

Verse 10. *King James version.* Hast thou not made an hedge about his house, and about all that he hath on every side? Thou has blest the work of his hands, and his substance is increased in the land.

Verse 10. *New version by Franklin.* Have you not protected him, and heaped your benefits upon him, till he is grown enormously rich?

Verse 11. *King James version.* But put forth thine hand now, and touch all that he hath, and he will curse thee to thy face.

Verse 11. *New version by Franklin.* Try him; only withdraw your favor, turn him out of his places, and withhold his pensions, and you will soon find him in the opposition.

This crime against beautiful letters was in perfect keeping with Franklin's general character. He had a cheap and shabby soul, and the upper levels of the mind were far beyond his reach. His one attempt at dignified philosophical speculation, "Dissertation on Liberty and Necessity" (1725), was so bad that even he was later ashamed of it. As for his scientific experiments, they have been vastly over-rated. "All that he invented was current supposition at the time; his work was rather in confirming and defining the scientific notions of others."

His writings enjoyed a vast popularity in his own day, and still do in ours, but that should not blind us to their inferior quality. All he had to say he borrowed from others, and what is worse, he was a bad borrower. The literature of England in the Seventeenth and Eighteenth Centuries was the most glorious in its entire history. There was the immortal King James version of the Bible, and there was the galaxy of stars beginning with Shakespeare and ending with Pope. Franklin read them all, but when he came to imitate and to borrow did he choose any of these? He rejected the entire lot, and instead picked "Poor Robin's Almanac"! And of the King James version his chief comment was that its style was "obsolete"!

To call Franklin "one of the greatest masters of English expression" is the veriest nonsense. Almost any one of the Eighteenth Century New England theo-logians wrote better. Franklin, to be sure, was easier to understand, but there was far less in him worth understanding. His influence on the national letters, in the long run, was probably nil. "He founded no school of literature. He gave no impetus to letters. He put his name to no great work of history, of poetry, of fiction."

But by his international prominence and by the wide circulation of his two-penny philosophy he left a lasting impression on the national culture. In him "the 'lowbrow' point of view for the first time took definite shape, stayed itself with axioms, and found a sanction in the idea of 'policy.'" Thrift, industry, and determination were essential virtues in the building of the nation, but they were not, then or at any other time in history, of sufficient human dignity to build a life philosophy on. Franklin did precisely that for his private life, and by the force of his personality did more than any other man in his day to graft it upon the American people. The vulgarity he spread is still with us.

D. H. Lawrence: BENJAMIN FRANKLIN

THE Perfectibility of Man! Ah heaven, what a dreary theme! The perfectibility of the Ford car! The perfectibility of which man? I am many men. Which of them are you going to perfect? I am not a mechanical contrivance.

Education! Which of the various me's do you propose to educate, and which do you propose to suppress?

Anyhow I defy you. I defy you, oh society, to educate me or to suppress me, according to your dummy standards.

The ideal man! And which is he, if you please? Benjamin Franklin or Abraham Lincoln? The ideal man! Roosevelt or Porfirio Diaz?

There are other men in me, besides this patient ass who sits here in a tweed jacket. What am I doing, playing the patient ass in a tweed jacket? Who am I talking to? Who are you, at the other end of this patience?

From *Studies in Classic American Literature* by D. H. Lawrence. Copyright 1923 by Thomas Saltzer, Inc., 1951 by Frieda Lawrence. Reprinted by permission of The Viking Press, Inc., New York.

Who are you? How many selves have you? And which of these selves do you want to be?

Is Yale College going to educate the self that is in the dark of you, or Harvard College?

The ideal self! Oh, but I have a strange and fugitive self shut out and howling like a wolf or a coyote under the ideal windows. See his red eyes in the dark? This is the self who is coming into his own.

The perfectibility of man, dear God! When every man as long as he remains alive is in himself a multitude of conflicting men. Which of these do you choose to perfect, at the expense of every other?

Old Daddy Franklin will tell you. He'll rig him up for you, the pattern American. Oh, Franklin was the first downright American. He knew what he was about, the sharp little man. He set up the first dummy American.

At the beginning of his career this cunning little Benjamin drew up for himself a creed that should "satisfy the professors of every religion, but shock none."

Now wasn't that a real American thing to do?

"That there is One God, who made all things."

(But Benjamin made Him.)

"That He governs the world by His Providence."

(Benjamin knowing all about Providence.)

"That He ought to be worshipped with adoration, prayer, and thanksgiving."

(Which cost nothing.)

"But—" But me not buts, Benjamin, saith the Lord.

"But that the most acceptable service of God is doing good to men."

(God having no choice in the matter.)

"That the soul is immortal."

(You'll see why, in the next clause.)

"And that God will certainly reward

virtue and punish vice, either here or hereafter."

Now if Mr. Andrew Carnegie, or any other millionaire, had wished to invent a God to suit his ends, he could not have done better. Benjamin did it for him in the eighteenth century. God is the supreme servant of men who want to get on, to *produce.* Providence. The provider. The heavenly store-keeper. The everlasting Wanamaker.

And this is all the God the grandsons of the Pilgrim Fathers had left. Aloft on a pillar of dollars.

"That the soul is immortal."

The trite way Benjamin says it!

But man has a soul, though you can't locate it either in his purse or his pocketbook or his heart or his stomach or his head. The *wholeness* of a man is his soul. Not merely that nice little comfortable bit which Benjamin marks out.

It's a queer thing, is a man's soul. It is the whole of him. Which means it is the unknown him, as well as the known. It seems to me just funny, professors and Benjamins fixing the functions of the soul. Why the soul of man is a vast forest, and all Benjamin intended was a neat back garden. And we've all got to fit in to his kitchen garden scheme of things. Hail Columbia!

The soul of man is a dark forest. The Hercynian Wood that scared the Romans so, and out of which came the white-skinned hordes of the next civilization.

Who knows what will come out of the soul of man? The soul of man is a dark vast forest, with wild life in it. Think of Benjamin fencing it off!

Oh, but Benjamin fenced a little tract that he called the soul of man, and proceeded to get it into cultivation. Providence, forsooth! And they think that bit of barbed wire is going to keep us in pound forever? More fools them.

This is Benjamin's barbed-wire fence. He made himself a list of virtues, which he trotted inside like a grey nag in a paddock.

1 TEMPERANCE Eat not to fulness; drink not to elevation.

2 SILENCE Speak not but what may benefit others or yourself; avoid trifling conversation.

3 ORDER Let all your things have their places; let each part of your business have its time.

4 RESOLUTION Resolve to perform what you ought; perform without fail what you resolve.

5 FRUGALITY Make no expense but to do good to others or yourself — i.e., waste nothing.

6 INDUSTRY Lose no time, be always employed in something useful; cut off all unnecessary action.

7 SINCERITY Use no hurtful deceit; think innocently and justly, and, if you speak, speak accordingly.

8 JUSTICE Wrong none by doing injuries, or omitting the benefits that are your duty.

9 MODERATION Avoid extremes, forbear resenting injuries as much as you think they deserve.

10 CLEANLINESS Tolerate no uncleanliness in body, clothes, or habitation.

11 TRANQUILLITY Be not disturbed at trifles, or at accidents common or unavoidable.

12 CHASTITY Rarely use venery but for health and offspring, never to dulness, weakness, or the injury of your own or another's peace or reputation.

13 HUMILITY Imitate Jesus and Socrates.

A Quaker friend told Franklin that he, Benjamin, was generally considered proud, so Benjamin put in the Humility touch as an afterthought. The amusing part is the sort of humility it displays. "Imitate Jesus and Socrates," and mind you don't outshine either of these two. One can just imagine Socrates and Alcibiades roaring in their cups over Philadelphian Benjamin, and Jesus looking at him a little puzzled, and murmuring: "Aren't you wise in your own conceit, Ben?"

"Henceforth be masterless," retorts Ben. "Be ye each one his own master unto himself, and don't let even the Lord put his spoke in." "Each man his own master" is but a puffing up of masterlessness.

Well, the first of Americans practised this enticing list with assiduity, setting a national example. He had the virtues in columns, and gave himself good and bad marks according as he thought his behaviour deserved. Pity these conduct charts are lost to us. He only remarks that Order was his stumbling block. He could not learn to be neat and tidy.

Isn't it nice to have nothing worse to confess?

He was a little model, was Benjamin. Doctor Franklin. Snuff-coloured little man! Immortal soul and all!

The immortal soul part was a sort of cheap insurance policy.

Benjamin had no concern, really, with the immortal soul. He was too busy with social man.

1 He swept and lighted the streets of young Philadelphia.

2 He invented electrical appliances.

3 He was the centre of a moralizing club in Philadelphia, and he wrote

the moral humourisms of Poor Richard.

4 He was a member of all the important councils of Philadelphia, and then of the American colonies.

5 He won the cause of American Independence at the French Court, and was the economic father of the United States.

Now what more can you want of a man? And yet he is *infra dig,* even in Philadelphia.

I admire him. I admire his sturdy courage first of all, then his sagacity, then his glimpsing into the thunders of electricity, then his common-sense humour. All the qualities of a great man, and never more than a great citizen. Middle-sized, sturdy, snuff-coloured Doctor Franklin, one of the soundest citizens that ever trod or "used venery."

I do not like him.

And, by the way, I always thought books of Venery were about hunting deer.

There is a certain earnest naïveté about him. Like a child. And like a little old man. He has again become as a little child, always as wise as his grandfather, or wiser.

Perhaps, as I say, the most complete citizen that ever "used venery."

Printer, philosopher, scientist, author and patriot, impeccable husband and citizen, why isn't he an archetype?

Pioneer, Oh Pioneers! Benjamin was one of the greatest pioneers of the United States. Yet we just can't do with him.

What's wrong with him then? Or what's wrong with us?

I can remember, when I was a little boy, my father used to buy a scrubby yearly almanack with the sun and moon and stars on the cover. And it used to prophesy bloodshed and famine. But also

crammed in corners it had little anecdotes and humorisms, with a moral tag. And I used to have my little priggish laugh at the woman who counted her chickens before they were hatched, and so forth, and I was convinced that honesty was the best policy, also a little priggishly. The author of these bits was Poor Richard, and Poor Richard was Benjamin Franklin, writing in Philadelphia well over a hundred years before.

And probably I haven't got over those Poor Richard tags yet. I rankle still with them. They are thorns in young flesh.

Because although I still believe that honesty is the best policy, I dislike policy altogether; though it is just as well not to count your chickens before they are hatched, it's still more hateful to count them with gloating when they *are* hatched. It has taken me many years and countless smarts to get out of that barbed-wire moral enclosure that Poor Richard rigged up. Here am I now in tatters and scratched to ribbons, sitting in the middle of Benjamin's America looking at the barbed wire, and the fat sheep crawling under the fence to get fat outside and the watchdogs yelling at the gate lest by chance anyone should get out by the proper exit. Oh America! Oh Benjamin! And I just utter a long loud curse against Benjamin and the American corral.

Moral America! Most moral Benjamin. Sound, satisfied Ben!

He had to go to the frontiers of his State to settle some disturbance among the Indians. On this occasion he writes:

We found that they had made a great bonfire in the middle of the square; they were all drunk, men and women quarrelling and fighting. Their dark-coloured bodies, half naked, seen only by the gloomy light of the bonfire, running after and beating one another with fire-brands, accompanied by their horrid yellings, formed a scene the most resembling our ideas of hell that could well be imagined. There was no appeasing the tumult, and we retired to our lodging. At midnight a number of them came thundering at our door, demanding more rum, of which we took no notice.

The next day, sensible they had misbehaved in giving us that disturbance, they sent three of their counsellors to make their apology. The orator acknowledged the fault, but laid it upon the rum, and then endeavoured to excuse the rum by saying: "The Great Spirit, who made all things, made everything for some use; and whatever he designed anything for, that use it should always be put to. Now, when he had made rum, he said: 'Let this be for the Indians to get drunk with.' And it must be so."

And, indeed, if it be the design of Providence to extirpate these savages in order to make room for the cultivators of the earth, it seems not improbable that rum may be the appointed means. It has already annihilated all the tribes who formerly inhabited the seacoast . . .

This, from the good doctor, with such suave complacency is a little disenchanting. Almost too good to be true.

But there you are! The barbed wire fence. "Extirpate these savages in order to make room for the cultivators of the earth." Oh, Benjamin Franklin! He even "used venery" as a cultivator of seed.

Cultivate the earth, ye gods! The Indians did that, as much as they needed. And they left off there. Who built Chicago? Who cultivated the earth until it spawned Pittsburgh, Pa.?

The moral issue! Just look at it! Cultivation included. If it's a mere choice of Kultur or cultivation, I give it up.

Which brings us right back to our question, what's wrong with Benjamin, that we can't stand him? Or else, what's wrong with us, that we find fault with such a paragon?

Man is a moral animal. All right. I am a moral animal. And I'm going to remain such. I'm not going to be turned into a virtuous little automaton as Benjamin would have me. "This is good, that is bad. Turn the little handle and let the good tap flow," saith Benjamin and all America with him. "But first of all extirpate those savages who are always turning on the bad tap."

I am a moral animal. But I am not a moral machine. I don't work with a little set of handles or levers. The Temperance-silence - order - resolution - frugality - industry - sincerity - justice - moderation - cleanliness - tranquillity - chastity - humility keyboard is not going to get me going. I'm really not just an automatic piano with a moral Benjamin getting tunes out of me.

Here's my creed, against Benjamin's. This is what I believe:

"That I am I."
"That my soul is a dark forest."
"That my known self will never be more than a little clearing in the forest."
"That gods, strange gods, come forth from the forest into the clearing of my known self and then go back."
"That I must have the courage to let them come and go."
"That I will never let mankind put anything over me, but that I will try always to recognize and submit to the gods in me and the gods in other men and women."

There is my creed. He who runs may read. He who prefers to crawl, or to go by gasoline, can call it rot.

Then for a "list." It is rather fun to play at Benjamin.

1 TEMPERANCE Eat and carouse with Bacchus, or munch dry bread with Jesus, but don't sit down without one of the gods.

2 SILENCE Be still when you have nothing to say; when genuine passion moves you, say what you've got to say, and say it hot.

3 ORDER Know that you are responsible to the gods inside you and to the men in whom the gods are manifest. Recognize your superiors and your inferiors, according to the gods. This is the root of all order.

4 RESOLUTION Resolve to abide by your own deepest promptings, and to sacrifice the smaller thing to the greater. Kill when you must, and be killed the same: the *must* coming from the gods inside you, or from the men in whom you recognize the Holy Ghost.

5 FRUGALITY Demand nothing; accept what you see fit. Don't waste your pride or squander your emotion.

6 INDUSTRY Lose no time with ideals; serve the Holy Ghost; never serve mankind.

7 SINCERITY To be sincere is to remember that I am I, and that the other man is not me.

8 JUSTICE The only justice is to follow the sincere intuition of the soul, angry or gentle. Anger is just, and pity is just, but judgment is never just.

9 MODERATION Beware of absolutes. There are many gods.

10 CLEANLINESS Don't be too clean. It impoverishes the blood.

11 TRANQUILLITY The soul has many motions, many gods come and go. Try and find your deepest issue, in every confusion, and abide by that. Obey the man in whom you recognize the Holy Ghost; command when your honour comes to command.

12 CHASTITY Never "use" venery at all. Follow your passional impulse, if it be answered in the other being; but never have any motive in mind, neither offspring nor health nor even pleasure, nor even service. Only know that "venery" is of the great gods. An offering-up of yourself to the very great gods, the dark ones, and nothing else.

13 HUMILITY See all men and women according to the Holy Ghost that is within them. Never yield before the barren.

There's my list. I have been trying dimly to realize it for a long time, and only America and old Benjamin have at last goaded me into trying to formulate it.

And now I, at least, know why I can't stand Benjamin. He tries to take away my wholeness and my dark forest, my freedom. For how can any man be free, without an illimitable background? And Benjamin tries to shove me into a barbed-wire paddock and make me grow potatoes or Chicagoes.

And how can I be free, without gods that come and go? But Benjamin won't let anything exist except my useful fellowmen, and I'm sick of them; as for his Godhead, his Providence, He is Head of nothing except a vast heavenly store that keeps every imaginable line of goods, from victrolas to cat-o'-nine tails.

And how can any man be free without a soul of his own, that he believes in and won't sell at any price? But Benjamin doesn't let me have a soul of my own. He says I am nothing but a servant of mankind — galley-slave I call it — and if I don't get my wages here below — that is, if Mr. Pierpont Morgan or Mr. Nosey Hebrew or the grand United States Government, the great US, US or SOMEOFUS, manages to scoop in my bit along with their lump — why, never mind, I shall get my wages HEREAFTER.

Oh Benjamin! Oh Binjum! You do NOT suck me in any longer.

And why oh why should the snuff-coloured little trap have wanted to take us all in? Why did he do it?

Out of sheer human cussedness, in the first place. We do all like to get things inside a barbed-wire corral. Especially our fellow-men. We love to round them up inside the barbed-wire enclosure of FREEDOM, and make 'em work. "*Work, you free jewel,* WORK!" shouts the liberator, cracking his whip. Benjamin, I will not work. I do not choose to be a free democrat. I am absolutely a servant of my own Holy Ghost.

Sheer cussedness! But there was as well the salt of a subtler purpose. Benjamin was just in his eyeholes — to use an English vulgarism meaning he was just delighted — when he was at Paris judiciously milking money out of the French monarchy for the overthrow of all monarchy. If you want to ride your horse to somewhere you must put a bit in his mouth. And Benjamin wanted to ride his horse so that it would upset the whole apple-cart of the old masters. He wanted the whole European apple-cart upset. So he had to put a strong bit in the mouth of his ass.

"Henceforth be masterless."

That is, he had to break-in the human ass completely, so that much more might be broken, in the long run. For the moment it was the British Government that had to have a hole knocked in it. The first real hole it ever had: the breach of the American rebellion.

Benjamin, in his sagacity, knew that the breaking of the old world was a long process. In the depths of his own under-consciousness he hated England, he hated Europe, he hated the whole corpus of the European being. He wanted to be American. But you can't change your nature and mode of consciousness like changing your shoes. It is a gradual shedding. Years must go by, and centuries must elapse before you have finished. Like a son escaping from the domination of his parents. The escape is not just one rupture. It is a long and half-secret process.

So with the American. He was a European when he first went over the Atlantic. He is in the main a recreant European still. From Benjamin Franklin to Woodrow Wilson may be a long stride, but it is a stride along the same road. There is no new road. The same old road, become dreary and futile. Theoretic and materialistic.

Why then did Benjamin set up this dummy of a perfect citizen as a pattern to America? Of course he did it in perfect good faith, as far as he knew. He thought it simply was the true ideal. But what we *think* we do is not very important. We never really know what we are doing. Either we are materialistic instruments, like Benjamin or we move in the gesture of creation, from our deepest self, usually unconscious. We are only the actors, we are never wholly the authors of our own deeds or works. IT is the author, the unknown inside us or outside us. The best we can do is to try to hold ourselves in unison with the deeps which are inside us. And the worst we can do is to try to have things our own way, when we run counter to IT, and in the long run get our knuckles rapped for our presumption.

So Benjamin contriving money out of the Court of France. He was contriving the first steps of the overthrow of all

Europe, France included. You can never have a new thing without breaking an old. Europe happens to be the old thing. America, unless the people in America assert themselves too much in opposition to the inner gods, should be the new thing. The new thing is the death of the old. But you can't cut the throat of an epoch. You've got to steal the life from it through several centuries.

And Benjamin worked for this both directly and indirectly. Directly, at the Court of France, making a small but very dangerous hole in the side of England, through which hole Europe has by now almost bled to death. And indirectly in Philadelphia, setting up this unlovely, snuff-coloured little ideal, or automaton, of a pattern American. The pattern American, this dry, moral, utilitarian little democrat, has done more to ruin the old Europe than any Russian nihilist. He has done it by slow attrition, like a son who has stayed at home and obeyed his parents, all the while silently hating their authority, and silently, in his soul, destroying not only their authority but their whole existence. For the American spir-

itually stayed at home in Europe. The spiritual home of America was and still is Europe. This is the galling bondage, in spite of several billions of heaped-up gold. Your heaps of gold are only so many muck-heaps, America, and will remain so till you become a reality to yourselves.

All this Americanizing and mechanizing has been for the purpose of overthrowing the past. And now look at America, tangled in her own barbed wire, and mastered by her own machines. Absolutely got down by her own barbed wire of shalt-nots, and shut up fast in her own "productive" machines like millions of squirrels running in millions of cages. It is just a farce.

Now is your chance, Europe. Now let Hell loose and get your own back, and paddle your own canoe on a new sea, while clever America lies on her muck-heaps of gold, strangled in her own barbed wire of shalt-not ideals and shalt-not moralisms. While she goes out to work like millions of squirrels in millions of cages. Production!

Let Hell loose, and get your own back, Europe!

Charles L. Sanford:
AN AMERICAN PILGRIM'S PROGRESS

A CONVENTIONAL rhetoric of spirit antedating Columbus' voyages of discovery helped to invest the new Western world and the way West with a magnetic attraction over European imaginations. It functioned to give the otherwise sordid pursuit of material riches moral and spiritual sanction, without which

most men seem disinclined to dare and do. This rhetoric revolved on the spiritual voyage or quest for personal salvation and reached its fullest literary expression in Dante's *Divine Comedy* and Bunyan's *Pilgrim's Progress*.

In the journey patterns of Scripture as well as in the language of medieval

From Charles L. Sanford, "An American Pilgrim's Progress," *American Quarterly*, Vol. IV (Winter, 1955). Printed with permission.

church symbolism, the spiritual quest had traditionally been known as a "journey toward light." According to this interpretation, if the bower of light was Paradise or the Celestial City, the original source of the bright beam was God, symbolized by the life-giving sun. The sun in medieval popular thought represented God's truth and righteousness, illuminating the dark corners of sin with His saving radiance in its solar cycle from East to West. Medieval fable with its strange wonders and miraculous beings had the kingdom of earthly desire located vaguely and variously in Abyssinia, in Cathay and Ophir, somewhere in the Far East, beyond the western seas. Medieval explorers sought out the warmest climes of the sun. But Christians, for the most part, looked for the promised land in the other world of life-after-death while they huddled in misery in this world. Anticipating the future importance of the direction West, Dante, in a famous passage from the *Divine Comedy*, has Ulysses sailing through the Straits of Gibraltar to reach the West, seeking "the new experience/ Of the uninhabited world behind the sun." Shouldering the dawn in the unknown western seas, Ulysses comes upon Mount Purgatory, where one begins the ascent to the Celestial City. Columbus, too, was saturated with medieval legend and thought literally that he had discovered "the terrestrial paradise."

But God's divine light did not shine everywhere with equal brilliance. "Wheresoever the children of Israel dwelt," Genesis maintained, "*there* was light." In other words, His brightest beams were reserved for God's elect, the chosen people. The Reformed Churches of Europe, under the leadership of Martin Luther, in effect revived the old Hebraic conception of a chosen people and claimed that the light of the true gospel

dwelt in their house. Since the Reformation rose first in the west of Europe and spread westward from Germany to France, the Netherlands, and thus to England, it became almost commonplace for the favored ones to suppose that the succession to the moral and spiritual leadership of the world followed the solar cycle of the sun from East to West. Settlement of the New World by militant Protestants completed the identification of geographical westering with moral and spiritual progress and, with the secularization of millennial hopes, contributed to the eighteenth- and nineteenth-century idea of progress.

Before and during the settlement of America the English considered themselves the custodians of the apostolic succession. Shakespeare's England was not only "this blessed plot, this earth, this realm"; it was also a bower of light, "this other Eden, demi-paradise, this fortress built by Nature" for a chosen people. On the eve of settlement, as Louis B. Wright has pointed out, Protestant theologians were frantically transferring the Ark of the Covenant from Abraham to the English. There were, undoubtedly, many laymen who cried with the Baptist Henry Nicholas, "We have it, we are the Congregation of Christ, we are Israel, lo here it is!" or with the Anglican William Crashaw, "The God of Israel is . . . the God of England." But there were also many Englishmen who were not loath to see the succession pass westward to America, so long as it redounded to the power and glory of England. Indeed, the English were divinely appointed to establish themselves in the promised lands of the New World! Thus, Richard Hakluyt urged in his *Discourse of Western Planting* that the western discoveries had provided England a heaven-sent opportunity for the spread of the gospel, "whereunto the Princes of the refourmed Relligion are chefely bounde." John White of Dorchester, author of *The Planters Plea,* considered England to be singled out for that work, "being of all the States that enjoy the libertie of the Religion Reformed" the most orthodox and sincere. As early as 1583 Sir Humphrey Gilbert thought England's "full possession of those so ample and pleasant countreys . . . very probable by the revolution and course of Gods word and religion, which from the beginning hath moved from the East, towards, and at last unto the West, where it is like to end. . . ."

The belief that the bounties of God followed the course of the sun westward brought numerous prophecies of a bright future for America and contributed, in part, to their fulfillment. Sir William Alexander, who was to become proprietor of Nova Scotia, wrote in 1616:

America to Europe may succeed;
God may stones raise up to Abram's seed.

The poet John Donne predicted in 1622 that the Virginia Company would make England a bridge between the Old World and the New "to join all to that world that shall never grow old, the kingdom of Heaven." A few years later another Anglican poet, George Herbert, noted in his *Church Militant* that

Religion stands tip-toe in our land
Ready to pass to the American strand.

Whereupon, Dr. Twiss, "considering our English Plantations of late, and the opinion of many grave divines concerning the Gospel's fleeing westward," asked his fellow clergyman, Mede —"Why may not that be the place of the new Jerusalem?" His question was later echoed by American colonists who founded cities in the wilderness and led periodic religious revivals on the frontier.

The image of a new Jerusalem in the western world accompanied dreams of empire and a higher civilization. Among the blessings which God had bestowed upon fallen reason, and whose great revival, according to seventeenth-century Chiliasts, was to usher in the last stage before the millennium, was culture and learning. "Learning, like the Sun," Thomas Burnet wrote in his *Archaeologiae* in 1692,

began to take its Course from the *East,* then turned *Westward,* where we have long rejoiced in its Light. Who knows whether, leaving these Seats, it may not yet take a further Progress? Or whether it will not be universally diffused, and enlighten all the World with its Rays?

The English Puritan divine, John Edwards, also traced the advance of culture and religion as a westward movement. In 1725 Jeremy Dummer, Massachusetts' agent in London, hoped, apropos of his collection of books for the new Yale library, that religion and polite learning would not rest in their westward progress until they took up their chief residence in America. Two years later Bishop Berkeley summed up for posterity ideas which had been in circulation for more than a century. His famous poem beginning, "Westward the course of empire takes its way," restated the familiar solar analogy to conform to the imperial vision of eighteenth-century Englishmen.

Although Englishmen transplanted in America shared this dream of imperial grandeur, they assumed a role for themselves which eclipsed that of the mother country and unconsciously hastened the separation of the colonies. They believed that they were the chosen instruments of God appointed to carry out the Protestant mission in the New World, which was to set up a "city on the hill" as an example to Europe and the rest of the world of the true Reformation. In this mission they regarded themselves as the heirs of all history, curiously unappreciated by Englishmen at home, for whose salvation they prayed. Their pre-eminence on the stage of history seemed guaranteed not only by the westward progression of religion and culture, but also by God's Providence in concealing America from European eyes until the time of the Reformation. There was little doubt in their minds that the final drama of moral regeneration and universal salvation was to begin here, with them.

This sense of unique destiny bred a religious patriotism which unwittingly started the colonists down the long road to political independence. The inner logic of their position was revealed by Thomas Paine, who on the eve of the American Revolution acknowledged the design of Heaven, adding, "The Reformation was preceded by the discovery of America, as if the Almighty graciously meant to open a sanctuary to the persecuted in future years. . . ." An incipient patriotism was also reflected, unconsciously to be sure, in the change in emphasis which many colonists, particularly New Englanders, gave to the conventional sun rhetoric. In the symbolic language of spirit they sometimes denied the sun its regular transit from East to West, and, instead, had it hovering or rising for the first time over them. As early as 1647 John Eliot, missionary to the Indians, was announcing "The Daybreaking if not the Sunrising of the Gospel . . . in New England." "O New-England," Samuel Willard hymned in a sermon of 1704, "thou art a Land of Vision; and has been so for a long time. The Sun for one day stood over Gibeon, so has the Sun of the Gospel been stand-

ing over us for Fourscore years together." The Sun of Righteousness, according to Jonathan Edwards, "shall *rise in the west,* contrary to the course of this world, or the course of things in the old heavens and earth." Such language implied a break with the European past. It is not surprising that Thomas Jefferson proposed as a Seal of State for the new nation a representation of the children of Israel led by a pillar of light, or that the goddess of liberty on our coins is flanked by a rising sun.

The chosen people of the American colonies looked upon their mission in the wilderness not merely as the continuation of something old, but as the beginning of something new: they were to usher in the final stage of history. They had inherited a new world in a physical sense, and in order "to vindicate the most rigorous ideal of the Reformation" they felt it necessary, as Jonathan Edwards said, "to begin a new world in a spiritual respect." Moreover, they associated their drama of moral and spiritual regeneration with a special plot of virgin land untouched by mistakes of the past and where failure was inexcusable. By national covenant with the children of Israel, God had appointed a promised land in Canaan. John Cotton told his people that they were the heirs of the covenant promise and that New England was the appointed place. Up and down the colonies, from Maine to Virginia, with a frequency suggesting that most colonists were, to a greater or less degree, touched by a sense of mission, colonists likened themselves to the tribes of Israel and called their country the "new Canaan," the "second Paradise," the "promised land," the "new heaven on earth." Not a few colonists, especially in New England, lived daily in agonized expectation of the Second Coming of Christ to America to inaugurate the millennium.

What the colonists did not realize was that, in tying their spiritual hopes to a plot of earth, they had already begun the process of what Carl Becker has called dismantling the celestial heaven in favor of an earthly one.

By the eighteenth century, piety had largely given way to moralism. But moralism continued to express a sense of mission and was intimately connected with the land. Just as the early frontier hardships had been held to be a test of the fitness of an Elect people in their incessant warfare against sin, so success in subduing the wilderness was tantamount to entering the kingdom of Heaven and seemed to demonstrate a direct causal relationship between moral effort and material reward. The opportunity for advancement afforded by the free lands of promise was contrasted to the static caste system of a Europe still fettered by feudalism. America's answer to Europe was now to rise in the economic scale by the application of industry, sobriety, and frugality, to improve upon the brutish state of nature, to carve out of the wilderness a pleasant land of rural villages, small shops, churches, and tilled fields — in short, to establish a superior civilization in which prosperity was the mark of special virtue. The process of moral regeneration was indeed a civilizing process, but, as opposed to the corrupt urban culture of Europe, the new American civilization was to have an agrarian basis, celebrating the simple virtues of the saw and the axe. The ultimate effect of the discovery of the new world was thus to substitute for the spiritual pilgrimage of Dante and Bunyan the "way West" as the way of salvation. It remained for an American Bunyan, Benjamin Franklin, to express the sense of this transformation in a moral fable which has gripped the imaginations of Americans ever since.

II

It would be rather easy to show that Benjamin Franklin was the product of eighteenth-century urban culture extending from Europe to colonial Boston and Philadelphia, that Franklin's Poor Richard had an affinity with the *Compleat Tradesman* of Daniel Defoe's England, and that therefore Franklin's moral virtues were broadly middle-class rather than peculiarly American. But such a view, whatever its merits, would overlook the fact that Americans, in response to a frontier environment and to a cyclical theory of history, have tended to emphasize the theme of moral regeneration in connection with the supposedly superior virtues of an agrarian civilization. The two most perceptive foreign observers of the nineteenth century, Alexis de Tocqueville and James Bryce, agreed in calling Americans as a whole the most moralistic and religious people in the world. The philosopher George Santayana once remarked that to be an American "is of itself almost a moral condition, an education, and a career," and in a similar tenor the expatriate Logan Pearsall Smith complained that Americans acted as if "America were more than a country, were a sort of cause."

A. Whitney Griswold has shown that Franklin's thirst for moral perfection was a distillation of the Protestant business ethic taught by Puritan ministers in Franklin's hometown of Boston. Franklin himself acknowledged the influence of Cotton Mather's "Essays to Do Good." Though the colonial urban culture opened to Franklin the opportunities for advancement, gave him access to the scientific and philosophic ideas of the Enlightenment, and enlisted him in projects for civic improvement, his moral vision was colored by the presence of the frontier. The colonial city, after all, rested on rural foundations. Cosmopolitan though he was, Franklin dreamed of a great agrarian utopia in which to preserve America's "glorious public virtue."

As early as 1753, when he was preoccupied with problems of Indian defense, he proposed, as a means both of enriching himself and strengthening the British empire, to settle a wilderness colony on the banks of the Ohio. "What a glorious Thing it would be," he wrote on that occasion, "to settle in that fine Country a large strong Body of Religious and Industrious People!" But his imperialistic vision of a greater England in the West reserved a special destiny for Americans which overshadowed the role of the mother country. He expressed this incipient patriotism in the sun and light imagery common to the rhetoric of westward expansion. " 'Tis said the Arts delight to travel Westward," he once remarked. He was long of the opinion "that the *foundations of the future grandeur and stability of the British empire lie in America.*" He playfully attributed a cosmic significance to the work of spiritual pioneering: "by *clearing America* of Woods" Americans were "*Scouring* our Planet, . . . and so making this Side of our Globe reflect a brighter Light to the Eyes of the Inhabitants in *Mars* or *Venus. . . .*" Franklin early identified the frontier with opportunity and tended to measure spiritual progress by progress in converting the wilderness into a paradise of material plenty.

A city-dweller, by profession a printer and tradesman, Franklin nevertheless located the true source of virtue in agricultural pursuits. "There seem to be but three ways for a nation to acquire wealth," he wrote, with an eye to the widening breach between England and the colonies. "The first is by *war*, as the Romans did, in plundering their conquered neighbours. This is *robbery*. The second by

commerce, which is generally *cheating*. The third by *agriculture*, the only *honest way*, wherein man receives a real increase of the seed thrown into the ground, in a kind of continual miracle. . . ." This was more than physiocratic doctrine; it was a program to keep a chosen people on the path of righteousness and prepare them for the moral and spiritual leadership of the earth. He made it clear that public morality was his special concern when he wrote after independence had been secured: "The vast Quantity of Forest Lands we have yet to clear, and put in order for Cultivation, will for a long time keep the Body of our Nation laborious and frugal." He repeatedly contrasted the vices of Europe and England with the "glorious public virtue" of America and habitually bestowed upon American farmers the ennobling title of "Cultivators of the Earth." By an outstanding example of good works, by his *Almanacks* and *Autobiography*, by his proposed *Art of Virtue* and by other writings, Franklin constituted himself chief guardian of the national conscience.

It has been said that Franklin's ethics were those of a tradesman and that the eighteenth-century concept of tradesman was English in origin. Yet an English writer, D. H. Lawrence, has found Franklin's archetypal new-world quality essentially in his moralism, and Herbert Schneider has written that, as a moralist, Franklin was "a child of the New England frontier." The truth is that the individualistic virtues of industry, frugality, and sobriety taught, if not always practiced, by Franklin, were adaptable to both the tradesman and farmer. Like the middle-class tradesman, the pioneer farmer was a small entrepreneur and capitalist, a speculator in land, a "cultivator," as Veblen has said, "of the main chance as well as of the fertile soil." The career of

Daniel Defoe, who died in obscurity and poverty, shows that Defoe spoke for a single class which was not yet able to break through the cramping restrictions of class and caste. Franklin spoke for a whole nation of middle-class *arrivistes*, but addressed himself particularly to the "Cultivators of the Earth" in opposition to the urban dwellers of the colonial city and of the European metropolis.

The American mission of moral regeneration derived its dynamism from the tension generated by the polarity between what the colonists considered an over-ripe stage of civilization in a Europe corrupted by feudal institutions and a simpler, agrarian society which more than made up in morals what it lacked in sophistication. American moralism implied a repudiation of European culture and of urbanism, though not a denial of the civilizing process. As the Revolution drew near, Franklin exaggerated the differences. From England he wrote to Joseph Galloway, who longed for a reconciliation, "When I consider the extream Corruption prevalent among all Orders of Men in this old rotten State, and the glorious publick Virtue so predominant in our rising Country, I cannot but apprehend more Mischief than Benefit from a closer Union." Political and military necessity demanded a smiling compliance with the ways of the world in Paris, where, among the powdered heads, he wore his fur cap as a native emblem; but he also had private reservations about the state of French culture. Occasionally his moral obsessions led him to flirt with a primitivism akin to the sentimental cult of the noble savage. Returning from a tour of Ireland and Scotland, he wrote:

. . . if my Countrymen should ever wish for the honour of having among them a gentry enormously wealthy, let them sell their Farms and pay rack'd Rents; the Scale of the Landlords will rise, as that of the Tenants is depresss'd, who will soon become poor, tattered, dirty, and abject in Spirit. Had I never been in the American colonies, but was to form my Judgment of Civil Society by what I have lately seen, I should never advise a Nation of Savages to admit of Civilization: For I assure you, that, in the Possession and Enjoyment of the various Comforts of Life, compar'd to these People every Indian is a Gentleman. . . .

In his identification of prosperity with virtue Franklin remembered that the covenant promise was with a whole people, not merely the few, and he wanted, as he said, "a general happy Mediocrity of fortune."

To be an American was to be a back-trailer to a more sophisticated society, in itself a moral condition. An aristocracy of wealth based on commerce and land speculation blossomed in the larger seaport towns of America. Rich Boston merchants thirsted after London, much as London aspired to Paris. Like Jefferson and many other Americans imbued with a sense of mission, Franklin did not want to see colonial urban centers emulate the class patterns of European society, and he, too, sometimes wished for an "ocean of fire" between the old world and the new. He transferred some of his animus against Europe to the coastal towns. "The People of the Trading Towns," he wrote at the end of the Revolution, "may be rich and luxurious, while the Country possesses all the Virtues, that tend to private Happiness and publick Prosperity. Those Towns are not much regarded by the Country; they are hardly considered as an essential Part of the States. . . . we may hope the Luxury of a few Merchants on the Seacoast will not be the Ruin of America." Franklin viewed with some alarm the social dislocations and misery caused by the new factory system in Europe. No more than Jefferson did he want to see Americans "twirling a distaff" in factories. Though he was the prophet of American technological efficiency, he did not anticipate industrialism. It may be supposed that his response to such urban problems as fire-fighting, poor street-lighting, pauperism, and improper sanitation was unconsciously motivated by a patriotic desire to avoid or mitigate the worst evils of urbanization.

Franklin's whole moral fiber was geared to raising a new man and a new society in the world of nations. Viewed in this light, his *Autobiography* is a great moral fable pursuing on a secular level the theme of John Bunyan's *Pilgrim's Progress*. There is little doubt of the serious intent underlying either the *Autobiography* or the creation of "Poor Richard," to impart moral instruction to the public. He wrote the *Autobiography*, as he said, to acquaint his posterity with the means of his success, "as they may find some of them suitable to their own situations, and therefore fit to be imitated." After breaking off the work, a friend persuaded him to continue it on the grounds that it would be useful to millions and would "lead the youth to equal the industry and temperance of thy early youth." Another friend urged its continuation "in conjunction with your Art of Virtue (which you design to publish) of improving the features of private character, and consequently of aiding all happiness, both public and domestic." Franklin originated *Poor Richard's Almanack* to make money, but, more importantly, to convey "instruction among the common people." He filled the calendar spaces "with proverbial sentences, chiefly such as inculcated industry and frugality, as the means of procuring wealth, and thereby securing virtue." Of late it has been popular to say with

Robert Spiller that "Poor Richard" was a humorous creation, never intended to be taken seriously. But Franklin's very humor was a vehicle for serious moral instruction and also expressed his sense of special destiny. Thus, his tall tales of sheep with tails so heavily laden with wool that they needed trailer-carts to carry them and of the whale which chased salmon up Niagara Falls, tales which anticipated the characteristic humor of the American frontier, were Franklin's way of whittling the urban sophisticate and European down to size and telling him, in effect, that things grew bigger and better in God's country.

The *Autobiography* is not simply a formless record of personal experience, or just a charming success story. Consciously or unconsciously, it is a work of imagination which, by incorporating the "race" consciousness of a people, achieves the level of folk myth. Franklin's biographer, Carl Van Doren, tells us that Franklin had no model for his kind of autobiography. This is not quite true. As a report on Franklin's spiritual progress in the new heaven on earth, the *Autobiography* in its basic dramatic form parallels Bunyan's great allegory. Franklin merely substituted, to use the phrase of Carl Becker, the secular story with a happy ending for the Christian story with the happy ending. *Pilgrim's Progress* was a best-seller in New England during the latter part of the seventeenth century. It admirably fitted the situation of a people whose feet were planted on the path to worldly success, but whose heads were still filled with visions of the Celestial City. Franklin's first book was *Pilgrim's Progress*, and his favorite author was John Bunyan. Franklin absorbed from the pages of *Pilgrim's Progress* lessons in artistry as well as confirmations for the new-world theme of moral regeneration. According to Frank-

BENJAMIN FRANKLIN AND THE AMERICAN CHARACTER
lin, Honest John was the first author whom he had met "who mixed narration and dialogue, a method of writing very engaging to the reader, who in the most interesting parts finds himself, as it were, brought into the company and present at the discourse." Franklin regarded Defoe's works as imitations of Bunyan in this respect. Franklin also combined narrative and dialogue in his *Autobiography* in order to convey the felt immediacy of his experience, but in relating Bunyan's theme to the details of his new environment he created an allegory of American middle-class superiority.

Franklin states his central organizing theme at the outset: his emergence "from the poverty and obscurity" in which he was born and bred "to a state of affluence and some degree of reputation in the world." He gives to this secular "rise" a moral and spiritual meaning discoverable in the special blessings of God. The boy entering Philadelphia with three loaves under his arm is obviously the prototype of Bunyan's Christian beginning his toilsome ascent to the Heavenly City. Franklin heightens the drama of his struggle upward against odds in his more worldly pilgrimage by reiterating the contrast between his humble beginnings and his improved station in life. Three times he halts his narrative at conspicuous points in order to recall to his readers the pathetic picture of his first arrival in Philadelphia. He frames the Philadelphia anecdote as carefully as if he were deliberately setting out to create an immortal legend. "I have been the more particular," he writes, "in this description of my journey, and shall be so of my first entry into the city, that you may in your mind compare such unlikely beginnings with the figure I have since made there." He would have the reader believe that his future wife, Deb-

orah Read, happened also to be present on that occasion to observe his unlikely beginnings.

Since his marriage is a marriage of convenience contributing to his rise in life, he associates the episode of the rolls with his courtship of Miss Read. Once established as an up-and-coming printer, he notes for the reader's convenience that he "made rather a more respectable appearance in the eyes of Miss Read than I had done when she first happened to see me *eating my roll* in the street." Though his success story is a triumph of moral individualism and personal salvation, he identifies it with the rise of a whole people. His rise in life thus parallels the growth of Philadelphia. After he has bought out his partner Meredith, there is a building boom: "whereas I remembered well, that when I first walked about the streets of Philadelphia, *eating my roll*, I saw most of the houses in Walnut Street . . . with bills on to be let. . . ." When, finally, he achieves world-wide fame by his electrical experiments, he confesses to being flattered by the honors heaped upon him: "for, *considering my low beginning*, they were great things to me." By now he has no need to mention the symbolic rolls.

Franklin's confessed *errata* are analogous to Christian's bundle of sins and to the giant Despair, over which he must prevail in order to gain the Heavenly City. Carl Van Doren has said that Franklin owed his success to "natural gifts of which Poor Richard could not tell the secret." But Franklin was not altogether without a sense of sin, and he believed that good works were the necessary means to personal salvation, or success. Obversely, as his attitude toward charity in the *Autobiography* indicates, he felt that failure to rise in life was the result of moral turpitude. Accordingly, in one of the most famous passages of the *Autobiography,* about the year 1728 Franklin "conceived the bold and arduous project of arriving at moral perfection." The important point is not that he failed, but that he tried and that the program of good works which he outlined here and elsewhere, in effect, completed the long process of dismantling the Celestial City. A tale by Nathaniel Hawthorne, "The Celestial Railroad," suggests an ironic inversion of Bunyan's original allegory. Franklin, in his pilgrimage towards the Heavenly City, sends his baggage ahead by postal service and sets up signposts for other travelers. He fills the Slough of Despond with Philadelphia cobblestones and almanacs. He lights the Valley of the Shadow of Death with street lamps. He smites Apollyon with a thunderbolt. He throws a bridge over the river Styx.

In the spiritual drama of a chosen people lay the source of that economic romanticism, so frequently confused with materialism, by which so many Americans have assumed a God-given right to the fruits of an Edenic tree. As Franklin said, "The Divine Being seems to have manifested his Approbation . . . by the remarkable Prosperity with which He has been pleased to favour the whole Country." Americans after Franklin would merely inherit the earth by presumption and without waiting for Divine Approbation. Franklin's motives for land speculation were not sordidly pecuniary, but included, as did his enthusiasm for science, a poetic conception of national destiny. Thus, he called his proposed colony on the Ohio the future "paradise on earth." The outbreak of the Revolution ended his petition to the Crown for western lands, but Americans came into a larger inheritance. To a great degree the American passion for liberty was an extension of the

passion to possess the earthly inheritance. This passion was not essentially economic, for Americans felt that they were enacting a spiritual pilgrimage in their westward trek towards light.

The spiritual longing of the colonists prepared the psychological foundations of the nineteenth-century concept of Manifest Destiny, which sanctioned American imperialism. Thus, Nathaniel Ames, Franklin's competitor in almanacs, predicted in 1758 that "As the celestial light of the gospel was directed here by the finger of God, . . . So arts and sciences will change the face of nature in their tour from hence over the Appalachian Mountains to the Western Ocean." After Franklin's death Americans who were disappointed with the results of coastal civilization pursued their special destiny inland, continuing to read the promise of American life in the westward cycle of the sun. At the height of westward expansion in the nineteenth century, Fourth of July orators often recaptured the old millennial fervor and were typically lyrical in sun worship:

Christianity, rational philosophy, and constitutional liberty, like an ocean of light are rolling their resistless tide over the earth. . . . Doubtless there may be partial revulsions. But the great movement will . . . be progressive, till the millennial sun shall rise in all the effulgence of universal day.

Americans refashioned for their own use a conventional rhetoric of spirit which had antedated the voyages of Columbus. For the millions who went west in their new-world version of "Pilgrim's Progress," the classic anecdote was the story of the poor boy who came to Philadelphia with three rolls under his arms and rose to fame and fortune.

Stuart P. Sherman: FRANKLIN AND THE AGE OF ENLIGHTENMENT

THE hero presented to the schoolboy and preserved in popular tradition is still an "uneducated tradesman of America": a runaway Boston printer, adorably walking up Market Street in Philadelphia with his three puffy rolls; directing his fellow shopkeepers the way to wealth; sharply enquiring of extravagant neighbours whether they have not paid too much for their whistle; flying his kite in a thunderstorm and by a happy combination of curiosity and luck making important contributions to science; and, to add the last lustre to his name, by a happy combination of industry and frugality making his fortune. This picturesque and racy figure is obviously a product of provincial America, — the first great Yankee with all the strong lineaments of the type: hardness, shrewdness, ingenuity, practical sense, frugality, industry, self-reliance.

The conception is perhaps sound enough so far as it goes, being derived mainly from facts supplied by Franklin himself in the one book through which he has secured an eternal life in literature. But the popular notion of his personality thus derived is incomplete, because the *Autobiography*, ending at the year 1757, contains no record of the thirty-three years which developed a competent provincial into an able, cultivated, and imposing man of the world.

The Franklin now discoverable in the ten volumes of his complete works is one of the most widely and thoroughly cultivated men of his age. He had not, to be sure, a university training, but he had what serves quite as well: sharp appetite and large capacity for learning, abundance of books, extensive travel, important participation in great events, and association through a long term of years with the most eminent men of three nations. The object of our colleges and universities is only to provide a feeble substitute for the advantages which Franklin enjoyed. In touch as printer and publisher with the classic and current literature produced at home and imported from abroad, he becomes in Philadelphia almost as good a "Queen Anne's man" as Swift or Defoe. His scientific investigations bring him into correspondence with fellow workers in England, France, Germany, Italy, Holland, and Spain. Entering upon public life, he is forced into coöperation or conflict with the leading politicians, diplomats, and statesmen of Europe. In his native land he has known men like Cotton Mather, Whitefield, Benjamin Rush, Benjamin West, Ezra Stiles, Noah Webster, Jay, Adams, Jefferson, and Washington. In England, where his affections strike such deep root that he considers establishing there his permanent abode, he is in relationship, more or less intimate, with Mandeville, Paine, Priestley, Price, Adam Smith, Robertson, Hume, Joseph Banks, Bishop Watson, the Bishop of St. Asaph, Lord Kames, Lord Shelburne, Lord Howe, Burke, and Chatham. Among Frenchmen he numbers on his list of admiring friends Vergennes, Lafayette, Mirabeau, Turgot, Quesnay, La Roche-

From "Franklin and the Age of Enlightenment" by Stuart Sherman in *The Cambridge History of American Literature* with the permission of the publishers, G. P. Putnam's Sons.

foucauld, Condorcet, Lavoisier, Buffon, D'Alembert, Robespierre, and Voltaire.

It is absurd to speak of one who has been subjected to the molding of such forces as a product of the provinces. All Europe has wrought upon and metamorphosed the Yankee printer. The man whom Voltaire salutes with a fraternal kiss is a statesman, a philosopher, a friend of mankind, and a favorite son of the eighteenth century. With no softening of his patriotic fibre or loss of his Yankee tang, he has acquired all the common culture and most of the master characteristics of the Age of Enlightenment, up to the point where the French Revolution injected into it a drop of madness: its emancipation from unscrutinized tradition and authority, its regard for reason and nature, its social consciousness, its progressiveness, its tolerance, its cosmopolitanism, and its bland philanthropy. . . . [Here follows a summary of Franklin's career which can be reconstructed from the Chronology at the beginning of this volume.]

It is perhaps in the field of politics that Franklin exhibits the most marked development of his power and his vision. A realistic inductive thinker, well versed in the rudiments of his subject long before the revolutionary theorists handled it, he was not rendered by any preconception of abstract rights indocile to the lessons of his immense political experience. He formulated his conceptions in the thick of existing conditions, and always with reference to what was expedient and possible as well as to what was desirable. He served his apprenticeship in the Philadelphia Junto Club, which at its inception was little more than a village improvement society, but which threw out branches till it became a power in the province, and a considerable factor in the affairs of the colonies. In this association

he learned the importance of cooperation, mastered the tactics of organization, practiced the art of getting propaganda afoot, and discovered the great secret of converting private desires into public demands. In proposing in 1754 his plan for a union of the colonies he was applying to larger units the principle of cooperative action by which he had built up what we might call today his "machine" in Pennsylvania. He had in too large measure the instincts and the ideas of a leader, and he had too much experience with the conflicting prejudices and the resultant compromises of popular assemblies, to feel any profound reverence for the "collective wisdom" of the people. "If all officers appointed by governors were always men of merit," he wrote in his *Dialogue Concerning the Present State of Affairs in Pennsylvania,* "it would be wrong ever to hazard a popular election." That his belief in popular representation was due as much to his sense of its political expediency as to his sense of its political justice is suggested by a passage in his letter on the imposition of direct taxes addressed to Governor Shirley, December 18, 1754: "In matters of general concern to the people, and especially where burthens are to be laid upon them, it is of use to consider, as well what they will be apt to think and say, as what they ought to think." His sojourn in England widened his horizons but not beyond the bounds of his nationality. As agent, he felt himself essentially a colonial Englishman pleading for the extension of English laws to British subjects across the sea, and playing up to the Imperial policy of crushing out the colonizing and commercial rivalry of France. The ultimate failure of his mission of reconciliation effected no sudden transformation of his political ideas; it rather overwhelmed him with disgust at the folly, the obstinacy, and the corruption rampant among English politicians of the period. He returned to the arms of his people because he had been hurled from the arms of his king, and he embraced their new principles because he was sure they could not be worse applied than his old ones. His respect for the popular will was inevitably heightened by his share in executing it in the thrilling days when he was helping his fellow countrymen to declare their independence, and was earning the superb epigraph of Turgot: *Eripuit fulmen coelo sceptrumque tyrannis.* His official residence in France completely dissolved his former antagonism to that country. In the early stages of the conflict his wrath was bitter enough towards England, but long before it was over he had taken the ground of radical pacificism, reiterating his conviction that "there is no good war and no bad peace." He who had financed the Revolution had seen too much non-productive expenditure of moral and physical capital to believe in the appeal to arms. If nations required enlargement of their territories, it was a mere matter of arithmetic, he contended, to show that the cheaper way was to purchase it. "Justice," he declared "is as strictly due between neighbor nations as between neighbor citizens, . . . and a nation that makes an unjust war is only a *great gang.*" So far as he was able, he mitigated the afflictions of noncombatants. He proposed by international law to exempt from peril fishermen and farmers and the productive workers of the world. He ordered the privateersmen under his control to safeguard the lives and property of explorers and men of science belonging to the enemy country; and he advocated for the future the abolition of the custom of commissioning privateers. In the treaty which he negotiated with Prussia he actually obtained the incorporation of an article so restricting the "zone of war" as to make a war between Prussia and the United States under its terms virtually impossible. His diplomatic intercourse in Europe had opened his eyes to the common interests of all pacific peoples and to the inestimable advantages of a general amity among the nations. His ultimate political ideal included nothing short of the welfare and the commercial federation of the world. To that extent, at least, he was a believer in majority interests! It may be further said that his political development was marked by a growing mastery of the art of dealing with men and by a steady approximation of his political to his personal morality.

For the broad humanity of Franklin's political conceptions undoubtedly his interest in the extension of science was partly responsible. As a scientific investigator he had long been a "citizen of the world," and for him not the least bitter consequence of the war was that it made a break in the intellectual brotherhood of man. If he had not been obliged to supply the army of Washington with guns and ammunition, he might have been engaged in the far more congenial task of supplying the British Academy with food for philosophical discussion. He could not but resent the brutal antagonisms which had rendered intellectual cooperation with his English friends impossible, and which had frustrated his cherished hope of devoting his ripest years to philosophical researches. A natural endowment he certainly possessed which would have qualified him in happier circumstances for even more distinguished service than he actually performed in extending the frontiers of knowledge. He had the powerfully developed curiosity of the explorer and the inventor, ever busily prying into the causes of things, ever speculating upon the consequences of novel combinations. His native inquisitiveness had been stimulated by a young civilization's manifold necessities, mothering manifold inventions, and had been supplemented by a certain moral and idealizing passion for improvement. The practical nature of many of his devices, his absorption in agriculture and navigation, his preoccupation with stoves and chimneys, the image of him firing the gas of ditch water or pouring oil on troubled waves, and the celebrity of the kite incident rather tend to fix an impression that he was but a tactful empiricist and a lucky dilettante of discovery. It is interesting in this connection to note that he confesses his lack of patience for verification. His prime scientific faculty, as he himself felt, was the imagination which bodies forth the shapes and relations of things unknown, which constructs the theory and the hypothesis. His mind was a teeming warren of hints and suggestions. He loved rather to start than to pursue the hare. Happily what he deemed his excessive penchant for forming hypotheses was safeguarded by his perfect readiness to hear all that could be urged against them. He wished not his view but truth to prevail — which explains the winsome cordiality of his demeanor towards other savants. His unflagging correspondence with investigators, his subscription to learned publications, his active membership in philosophical societies and his enterprise in founding schools and academies all betoken his prescience of the wide domain in which science had to conquer and of the necessity for cooperation in the task of subduing it. Franklin was so far a Baconian that he sought to avoid unfruitful speculation and to unite contemplation and action in a stricter embrace for the generation of knowledge useful to man. But in refutation of any charge that he was a narrow-minded utilitarian and lacked the liberal views and long faith of the modern scientific spirit may be adduced his stunning retort to a query as to the usefulness of the balloons then on trial in France: "What is the use of a new born baby?"

Herbert W. Schneider: UNGODLY PURITANS

NOT long after the appearance of Cotton Mather's *Essays to Do Good,* the readers of the *New England Courant* were startled by the satirical articles of one Mrs. Silence Dogood. She agreed with the Reverend Mr. Mather that doing good was the most important business of life; but she made it her business to expose evil in high places. She began by attacking college life among the "scollars" at Harvard; then she reprimanded their parents for sending them merely to display their own wealth; then she made fun of the theological debates and pretensions of the professors. The fashionable clergy came in for their share of moral treatment by Mrs. Dogood, and even the magistrates and members of the council were not spared. Such essays to do good were not exactly to the Mathers' taste and, when James Franklin, the editor of the *Courant,* and Silence Dogood, whose real name was Benjamin Franklin, continued in their efforts despite warnings, fines and

From *The Puritan Mind* by Herbert Wallace Schneider. Copyright, 1930, by Henry Holt and Company, Inc. Used by permission of the publishers.

imprisonment, their journal was finally suppressed.

Removed to Philadelphia, Benjamin continued to "do good." When he organized his Junto Club there, he inserted among the rules of procedure the following paraphrases of Cotton Mather's proposals: "Have you lately observed any encroachment on the just liberties of the people? What new story have you lately heard agreeable for telling in conversation? Have you lately heard of any citizen thriving well, and by what means? Do you think of anything at present, in which the Junto may be serviceable to mankind, to their country, or to themselves?" Between these queries there was a pause "while one might fill and drink a glass of wine," in place of Cotton Mather's pause "that any member may offer what he pleases upon it."

In all this there was evidently an element of sheer wit and playfulness. Franklin had caught the spirit of Addison and Steele's *Spectator*, of Defoe's *Essays*, and in general of the free-thinking, satirical literature of his day. In company with his young deistic friends, first in Boston, then in Philadelphia, and later in London, he enjoyed the free play of radical ideas. During his first sojourn in London he published a tract *On Vice and Virtue*, which proved that on the premises of God's attributes of wisdom, goodness, and power, one is forced to conclude that "vice and virtue are empty distinctions." A few years later he used the same sort of reasoning on prayer and predestination. Franklin's own summary of it appeared in a letter to Vaughan in 1779. "Almost all men, in all ages and countries, have at times made use of prayer. Thence I reasoned, that, if all things were ordained, prayer must among the rest be ordained. But, as prayer can procure no change in things ordained, praying must

be useless, and an absurdity. God would therefore, not ordain praying, if everything else was ordained. But praying exists, therefore all things are not ordained, &c."

At first, in his eagerness to be counted one of the clever deistic intellectuals, he concluded from such considerations that morality did not exist. In care-free fashion he exploited the arguments of both Calvinists and Deists. He wrote a *Dissertation on Liberty*, one on *First Principles*, and some *Dialogues Concerning Virtue and Pleasure*. These pieces all reveal a fondness for pushing an argument to its limits; they are not moralistic but sheer free-thinking. Soon, however, Franklin abandoned this speculative and playful tone and emphasized the more serious implications of the business of doing good. He discovered that the arguments in which he and his comrades indulged were merely continuing the bad intellectual habits of the theologians. Here is his own confession and condemnation of his early disputatious habits: "We sometimes disputed, and very fond we were of argument, and were desirous of confuting one another — which disputatious turn is apt to become a very bad habit, making people often disagreeable in company, by the contradiction that is necessary to bring it into practice; and thence, besides souring and spoiling the conversation, it is productive of disgusts, and perhaps enmities, with those who may have occasion for friendship. I had caught this by reading my father's books of dispute on religion. Persons of good sense, I have since observed, seldom fall into it, except lawyers, university men, and generally men of all sorts, who have been bred at Edinburgh."

From this it appears that one reason why Franklin abandoned dialectical and theological disputes was his desire to be well-mannered. He noticed that "positiveness" and "direct contradiction" were not in good taste in polite conversation. Accordingly he disciplined himself and imposed fines on members of the Junto who committed these violations of good manners.

There is a more serious reason, however, for Franklin's so-called conversion from Deism. His own hard experiences and his whole New England training convinced him that vice and virtue were "no empty distinctions" and that the theologies and metaphysics which made them appear such were therefore futile. This discovery he mentions in the *Autobiography* with his characteristic simplicity. "I grew convinced that truth, sincerity and integrity, in dealings between man and man, were of the utmost importance to the felicity of life." He realized that the liberal theologians and the city churches were relaxing from the gospel of work and discipline which the Puritans had preached during the generations of strenuous building, and were becoming acclimated to the habits of luxury and leisure. The spirit of work was giving way to the theology of having arrived, and the clergy were degenerating into a disputatious crowd of theocrats. Meanwhile more secular workers were exemplifying the strenuous virtues of the early Puritans. In this situation, Benjamin Franklin made the attempt to maintain the Puritan virtues in all their rigor, but to abandon entirely their theological sanctions. He placed the frontier morality on a utilitarian footing, and gave it empirical foundations. The whole issue he put in a few words: "Revelation had indeed no weight with me, as such; but I entertained an opinion, that, though certain actions might not be bad, *because* they were forbidden by it, or good, *because* it commanded them; yet probably these actions

might be forbidden *because* they were bad for us, or commanded *because* they were beneficial to us, in their own natures, all the circumstances of things considered." What Franklin said was simply: If you want to achieve anything, these old-fashioned Puritan virtues are the necessary means: temperance, silence, order, resolution, frugality, industry, sincerity, justice, etc. And if you ask for proof, Franklin could point to his own experience and to the colonies themselves as evidence.

What is designated as the Benjamin Franklin morality is probably too familiar to require detailed description. . . . [Here follows an account of Franklin's project for arriving at moral perfection, together with a listing of Franklin's moral precepts.]

Philosophers are offended by the simplicity, almost simpleness, of this morality. Surely there can be nothing profound in a doctrine which a Pennsylvania farmer could understand. Though more recent instrumentalists have succeeded in putting this doctrine in language which appeals more to "university men, and generally men of all sorts that have been bred at Edinburgh," any analysis of intelligence usually reveals the validity of Franklin's contentions; and though it may be more systematically developed and more elaborately conceived, the implications for conduct will be substantially the same. Certainly no method of presentation of utilitarian ethics could have been more effective than Franklin's, for he is to this day the patron saint of those who are interested in achievement.

Franklin's mind is typical of an easy, spontaneous hospitality to ends or ideals, and of an intellectual preoccupation with their practical challenge. Pennsylvania needed fortification against the French and Indians; Franklin began at once to work on plans for organizing a militia and buying cannon. In view of their common interests against Great Britain, the colonies wanted some sort of union; Franklin immediately proposed a plan. Throughout his life, he was continually proposing plans — a plan for the promotion of abolition of slavery, a plan for bringing the comforts of civilization to the natives of New Zealand. The "art of virtue" was simply one more plan. Any end, suggested to his mind, immediately raised the problem of its accomplishment. He even told the great evangelist, George Whitefield, how he could most easily convert great numbers of people, advising him to convert a few popular leaders, "grandees," first and then the masses would follow. "For," said he, "men fear less the being in hell than out of fashion." In his scientific researches, too, practical problems seemed to stimulate him most. I do not mean practical applications like the lightning-rod, for these were of minor concern to him, but rather problems of designing apparatus, of experimental conditions for testing hypotheses, and of methods for dealing pragmatically with rival hypotheses. His inventions are further evidence of this habit of mind — an improved harmonica of vibrating glasses, bi-focal spectacles, smokeless fireplaces, to say nothing of his electrical devices. It would be difficult to find a mind more given to free play in the objects of its interests, yet more intent on their practical aspects.

In his preoccupation with instrumental values, Franklin is typical of what Europeans call "Americanism," and the objection usually made to Franklin's moral philosophy, and for that matter to any other utilitarian ethics, is that it is merely instrumental. "You tell us," the criticism runs, "the 'way to wealth,' but you fail to tell us whether or not wealth is a good. You tell us how to succeed in business,

but you fail to tell us whether or not our business is worth while." The more superficial critics of Franklin (to say nothing of the critics of utilitarianism and pragmatism) immediately infer that "material prosperity" is the admitted end. To them Franklin is merely a typical American business man who, without stopping to evaluate, simply adopts the business principles of thrift for thrift's sake, money for money's sake, the more the better. That this is not true of Franklin's personal life is easily proved. As soon as he became "free and easy" he quit his business and devoted himself to science, literature, public affairs, and conversation with his friends, — pursuits which from boyhood had been his chief delight. As early as 1748 he wrote to Cadwallader Colden: "I am in a fair way of having no other tasks than such as I shall like to give myself, and of enjoying what I look upon as a great happiness, leisure to read, study, make experiments, and converse at large with such ingenious and worthy men as are pleased to honor me with their friendship or acquaintance, on such points as may produce something for the common benefit of mankind, uninterrupted by the little cares and fatigues of business." And a year later he wrote to his mother: "At present I pass my time agreeably enough. I enjoy, through mercy, a tolerable share of health. I read a great deal, ride a little, do a little business for myself, now and then for others, retire when I can, and go into company when I please; so the years roll round, and the last will come, when I would rather have it said, 'He lived usefully,' than 'He died rich.'" A further example of this attitude is found in his speculations on "raising a United Party for Virtue." The successful demonstration of his "art of virtue" on himself suggested to him the possibilities of its social and political application. Members of this

United Party, "good and wise men" of all nations, were to discipline themselves in accordance with the program Franklin had earlier followed himself. They were to be called "The Society of the Free and Easy. Free, as being, by the general practice and habits of the virtues, free from the dominion of vice; and particularly, by the practice of industry and frugality, free from debt, which exposes a man to constraint, and a species of slavery to his creditors."

Mr. D. H. Lawrence's criticism of Franklin's table of virtues rests entirely on his presupposition that they are final, not instrumental virtues. If they are taken as the ends of life, they are easily satirized. Lawrence himself seems to fall into the trap which he lays for Franklin in that he tries to re-define these purely disciplinary virtues in such a way as to give them ideal content. The result is even more ridiculous than it is intended to be. Justice, for example, he re-defines as follows: "The only justice is to follow the sincere intuition of the soul, angry or gentle. Anger is just, and pity is just, but judgment is never just." This is obviously no definition of justice at all. It may be a definition of freedom. Lawrence was so preoccupied with the praise of freedom, of individuality, of mastery, of imagination, of his gods, in short, of the ideal or final values of life, that it never occurred to him that Franklin could be talking about something quite different. Franklin's table of virtues is not a catalogue of his ideals or objects of worship, and to attempt to read ideal content into them is Lawrence's, not Franklin's, mistake. Franklin was just as much interested in being "free and easy" as Lawrence was — more so, in fact, for he was willing to work towards it. No one can blame Lawrence for protesting against the popular confusion of means and ends, and the general

tendency to make God an "everlasting Wanamaker," but his reading this into Franklin himself is not excusable. Lawrence seems to have had a fairly keen appreciation of ideals, but none whatsoever of morals; Franklin had some of both. "Early to bed and early to rise, makes a man healthy, wealthy and wise." Health, wealth, and wisdom, is not a bad summary of the final goods of human life. But none of them occur in Franklin's table of virtues; it is concerned exclusively with the "early to bed and early to rise" side of life. Lawrence had no room for this instrumental side of life in his philosophy, but one suspects that even he, as a matter of practice, applied considerable "resolution, frugality, industry and sincerity" to the writing of his books, though, as an artist, he had the good taste not to talk about it.

In Franklin's philosophy, as well as in his personal life, therefore, a sense of values is evident, values of which he did not lose sight, and in the service of which his moral philosophy was merely and precisely an instrument. Franklin was not interested in establishing his Puritan discipline as an end in itself. He assumed that people have ends, that they want to be "free and easy," and that they understand wealth as merely the necessary means for enjoying the real ends of leisure society. The reason "wealth" and similar terms figured so largely in Franklin's writings was simply that the people for whom he was writing thought in those terms. Any term which symbolized the ends for which people actually were striving was welcome to Franklin. He made no attempt to prescribe the ends which men should follow.

Franklin's attention was as consistently confined to the concrete analysis of means as the attention of the Greeks to ends. Aristotle made explicit what any Greek would have admitted to be a life well lived. The greatness of his ethics rests on the fact that the Greek virtues, — balance, wisdom, beauty, and the rest, — are commonly admitted ends. Franklin's virtues, —frugality, industry, sincerity, honesty, and the rest, — are not ends. It was the glory of the Greeks that they persisted in painting perfection in the face of practically minded objectors, with their, "But how is this possible in a barbarian world?" It was the greatness of Franklin, on the other hand, that he refused to abandon his Puritan principles because they were disagreeable. The decline of Puritan morals symbolizes less a growing tolerance of natural goods, or a discovery of better methods of attaining them, than an impatience at being obliged to work for them. The freedom, leisure and beauty which we enjoy are obviously the fruit of generations of discipline and even of slavery, and while we do well to point out the slavishness of those Puritans who make discipline an end in itself, we are in danger of the folly of imagining that we can achieve beauty without labor. The Greeks took slavery for granted. We, too, would be nearer the facts of life if we took slavery for granted, than we are when we imagine that Puritan virtues are antiquated. They are as universal in morals as the Greek ideals are in art. Their truth is as old as history and quite proverbial. It was understood long before Franklin, but seldom has it been stated so concretely, so simply, and so empirically. The hypothetic form of these maxims is indicative of their scientific character. They do not dictate, they advise. Franklin does not say, "thou shalt and thou shalt not." He says, "*if* you would be healthy, wealthy and wise, you must go early to bed and be early to rise; *if* you would be free and easy you must cultivate the art of virtue;

etc." Judgments in this form are about matters of fact and can be put to empirical tests. Not being bound to a particular set of standards, such an inquiry can discover the physical conditions of any. An ethics of means is, therefore, akin to the sciences, as an ethics of ends is to the arts. Artists are engaged each in his own individual work, but the instruments with which they ply their arts may be common. Or, in Franklin's own terms, the art of virtue may be useful to anyone for whom life is an art.

Franklin's table of virtues, inasmuch as it is not a philosophy of human ideals, is to be regarded neither as a substitute for the Aristotelian ethics, nor as a glorification of bourgeois commercialism in the face of the chivalry of the feudal aristocracy. If the Franklin morality substitutes for anything, it is for the traditional Christian virtues, for they, too, constitute a philosophy of the discipline of life. The Christian life is traditionally portrayed as one of humility, charity, penitence, poverty, self-denial, a forgiving spirit. These are obviously instrumental virtues and not ideal perfections, for they disappear in heaven. This traditional code of the feudal ages proved ill-adapted to the pioneer life of New England. Consequently the Puritan virtues, in spite of the fact that they were sanctioned by a Christian theology, were not traditionally Christian. The contrast between the Yankee and the saint, as types of character, is familiar enough. The two philosophies involved are practical alternatives. Franklin, in the *Autobiography*, explicitly retracts humility, the chief of the Christian virtues, as impractical; he said he found that when he was humble he was proud of his humility, and he admitted that he had hastily inserted humility as the thirteenth virtue in his table on the advice of a Quaker who told him that he "was generally thought proud."[1] Franklin's diagnosis of his own case corresponds fairly well to the historians' diagnosis of Puritans in general. They pretended to live saintly lives, but their actual ideals were pagan. They pursued "health, wealth and wisdom" while they professed election into the Covenant of Grace. Franklin saw clearly the growing incompatibility between the morals practiced and the morals preached, and he changed the preaching.

There was a brief time in Franklin's life when he concerned himself more or less seriously with religious reform. He tried to work out in detail a religious system which would give sincere expression to his moral ideas. He wrote down the rudiments of a theology, composed prayers, and while in England he even undertook, with Lord le Despencer, to revise the English Prayer Book. For various reasons he soon abandoned this project. To a certain extent Freemasonry and his Junto Club were his substitutes for churches. But above all he dropped religious subjects in order not to stimulate one more theological controversy. He made it a policy to disturb no one in his religious

practices and beliefs; he supported various religious institutions and he apparently became a good friend of both Whitefield and Samuel Johnson. Thus he made his peace with all religions and devoted himself to none. And while theologians were struggling, as we have seen, to revise Christian ideas to meet changing American morals, Franklin was free to take the other alternative. He reasserted the stern Puritan morality, but divorced it from the theocratic aims which it originally served.

In his austere moralism, Franklin was undoubtedly a Puritan, however much he may have revolted against Calvinism. His "art of virtue" is in significant contrast to the liberal temper and popular radicalism of his day and it can not be regarded as the product of his contacts with European civilization, nor of his Freemasonry, nor of his admiration for Sir Roger de Coverley. In other ways Franklin was no doubt a typical eighteenth-century man of the world, but as a moralist he was a child of the New England frontier. Jonathan Edwards and Benjamin Franklin thus represent the two opposite poles of Puritan thought. It was Edwards who attempted to induce New England to lead a godly, not a sober, life; it was Franklin who succeeded in teaching Americans to lead a sober and not a godly life.

---

[1] Compare Jonathan Edwards' remark that he was not content to be merely humble to the dust as other sinners are, but infinitely humble!

I. Bernard Cohen: THE EMPIRICAL TEMPER

AS an expression of the American character, Franklin spoke with the personality of his own genius, but the particular qualities of the American character that he represented were also the results

of the time and place in which he lived. He was a product of the philosophies of the eighteenth century, but he also came out of an American background — in Boston and Philadelphia — that conditioned the way he thought and that gave him a view of man and nature that stamped his contributions to our American way of life with a mark of its own. To define exactly what Franklin was, and to grasp in its full integrity what it is that Franklin stands for, we must pause to examine the wellsprings of that blend of idealism and practicality that he displayed.

It is true, of course, that even when we emulate Franklin, or address ourselves to problems of business, government and society in the Franklinian manner, we do so from a motivation that is apt to be somewhat different from his. Yet, even though two centuries of time and culture intervene between him and us, there are elements in his general approach to the world that have appeared again and again in Americans from his day to ours. Franklin's orientation is most easily discernible in the field of action in which he made the most original contribution — science — and so we may best see him in his own terms by first exploring the qualities of mind he displayed in studying nature and only then seeing how these qualities illuminate his way through life.

It has become commonplace to say that Benjamin Franklin was a practical man and to imply that his standard of value was always the working usefulness of the end result rather than the means of obtaining it or the motivation. We think of Franklin as having been primarily a practical man because so many of his enterprises were successful and because he had a doctrine of "usefulness" that seems akin to practicality. But in thus limiting Benjamin Franklin, we fail to grasp his full dimensions and may even slight our own national character. For there is a sense in which practicality implies expediency, and its ascription to the American character would rob our history of the lofty ideals and high purposes which have motivated so many of our leaders and our ordinary citizens; it would make a parody of Franklin as a guide through life.

As a man of the eighteenth century and an American, Benjamin Franklin was an empiricist. The America of his day was a young country in which a man's courage, faith, optimism or ability counted for nothing if he could not recognize and face up to the raw facts of life and nature. Franklin was not a product of the frontier in that he was an urban American, spending his boyhood in the city of Boston and his young manhood in the city of Philadelphia; he did not grow up in a log cabin in the wilderness, tilling fields with a flintlock by his side. But the spirit of the frontier certainly made its presence known in Philadelphia: the city itself was rough, unfinished and growing; there were Indian alarms not far away and a threat of pirates; and, in general, a spirit of building and material creation produced an atmosphere of close contact with the real world.

Nature, as Franklin realized, is both man's enemy and friend, providing fertile soil and rain and also plagues of insects and droughts. The only way to master Nature is to understand her laws and to operate within her framework. Shaking a fist at the skies will neither make it rain nor stop the locusts, although in Franklin's day men believed that prayer and fasting might do both. But the men who had braved the wilderness, although placing their reliance on their prayer book and Bible, knew that their faith in God needed to be buttressed by hard work and skill in shooting muskets. The Old World patterns of life, in which a man lived like his father and his father's father before him, could not long survive in the New World, where a man had to adapt himself to the realities of the situation in which he found himself, to find a way of life consistent with the data of experience that made up the external environment. It is this last quality which is the primary ingredient of empiricism: a respect for the data of experience and the application of reason to them.

In Benjamin Franklin this strain of empiricism enabled him to become a foremost scientist of that age, and it was a major factor in producing that special view of man, his needs, his rights and his works which has become so precious an element in our American heritage. Franklin stands in the American tradition for the proposition that reflections about society should produce useful institutions for the improvement of the conditions of life; considerations about the estate of man should yield more than eternal principles and noble concepts, and must be fruitful of a system of government and laws to safeguard man's rights; an understanding of the nature and character of man should lead to conduct that respects a man for what he is without regard to color or religion or economic and social origin. Many Americans have acted in accordance with these principles simply because they have become a part of our American pattern of behavior, but in Franklin they were a result of the brand of empiricism that marked his thought and conduct. To see Franklin's particular contribution to America, therefore, we must try to understand how being a good scientist and being a good neighbor, friend and citizen were but different aspects of a single fundamental quality of mind.

Empiricism is a philosophy which is of the eighteenth century and may be studied in Locke, whom Franklin respected, and Hume, whom Franklin knew and admired. One of its major tenets was the theory of how ideas originate in the mind by the action of sensations. Skeptical of any sort of metaphysics, Franklin was not a systematic philosopher, and doctrines of the origin of ideas held no great interest for him. Even so, throughout his writings we find a tendency to regard experience as the grand source of values and doctrines. He was certainly an empiricist in the sense that he considered an experiential test more important in evaluating the worth of concepts than their logical consistency or their mutual relatedness in a system.

Franklin's outlook demanded that concepts be founded on experience, whether that experience was the data of experiment in the laboratory or the observation of man's behavior. Reason, operating on these concepts, discovers laws of nature or rules of conduct, which must meet two important tests. First, these laws or rules or principles must be true — that is, they must be testable against that same experience of the laboratory or the world. But even if such an experiential test reveals the validity of the discovered generalization, the whole effort is not worth while unless it is productive of something new. It is this quality of productivity that gives man the final measure of the way in which the initial data and the reasoning process have led to the final conclusions.

Real works are thus, as Bacon put it, the fruits of knowledge and it is in this sense that he wrote that the roads to knowledge and to power are the same. For in the empiricist philosophy the end product can be no more divorced from real experience than the original concepts. In science, then, an empiricist begins by making experiments with his own hands, then constructing concepts that are related to the actual operations or manipulations he performs; next he applies his reason to generalize what he has observed into ground principles on which a logical theory can be built; then the final result is a new form of experience or at least a new view of some segment of experience.

One result of empirical science is a prediction, such as Newton made, of the tides; the time of tides was observable to anyone, but up until the time of Newton no one had understood the attractions of the sun and moon sufficiently well to explain how they might control the seas. Newton's predictions agreed so well with observation that the validity of his theory was assured. Newton's work led to predictions which were testable by experience and it contributed to an enlarged view of the world that we observe around us, thus being doubly productive. Sometimes the end product of empirical science is a new effect or phenomenon that the scientist can produce with his own hands in the laboratory, but often it is a new instrument or device which is itself the new experience that is the product or fruit of investigation.

As a scientist Franklin knew that the life of ideas in science is always controlled by experiment and observation and that a new theory such as he created is valuable in correlating phenomena that had not been thought related or in predicting new phenomena which, on being discovered, would prove the theory's usefulness. Applying his new concepts of electrical equilibrium and the states of electrification he called "plus" or "positive" and "minus" or "negative," Franklin discovered the first exact law of electricity: the law of conservation of charge. This occurred in the course of his experiments to analyze the charge in a condenser — the Leyden jar, consisting of a glass bottle coated on the outside with metal foil and filled with water or bird shot. Such an instrument, when charged, was capable of giving a noticeable shock to seven hundred men, but Franklin stated

that there was no more "electricity" in a charged jar than an uncharged one and he proved it by the experiment of "electrical convection." He also found that the charge "resided" in the nonconducting glass rather than the metal coat or water. But this led immediately to the production of new experience, because if charge "resides" in glass because glass is a special kind of nonconductor, then a condenser need not have the shape of a bottle, but could be made of glass plates with metal sheets affixed to either side. To the nonscientist this example may appear trivial, but it marked the beginning of condenser design and the condenser is one of the vital organs of every piece of electronic equipment ever made.

Furthermore, one of Franklin's greatest achievements was to show which electrical properties of bodies depend on their shape and which do not. Franklin never saw any practical use in the condenser, by which I mean that in his day the Leyden jar was never embodied in an instrument to serve man's needs or increase his fortune. Franklin's explanation of the condenser's action, we may note, was considered by his contemporaries to have been one of his major contributions to science; this discovery was useful because it increased man's understanding of nature's operations and it was productive because it led to new principles or laws of nature.

The distinction between productive usefulness and practicality may best be illustrated by Franklin's research on the lightning discharge. Having discovered that a pointed conductor will "draw off" the charge from an electrified body at a considerable distance, and having at last understood the role of grounding and insulation in electrostatic experiments, Franklin was in a position to make the grand experiment. If clouds are (as he thought) electrified, then an elevated vertical metal rod ending in a point will "draw off" some of the charge from low clouds though they are far away. This original experiment, described by Franklin and performed according to his specifications before he had thought of the kite experiment, established as an empirical fact the phenomenon that clouds are electrically charged and that lightning is therefore an electrical discharge. So the facts of experience and a theory based on correct reasoning had been productive of new experience; nature's artillery had been shown to be only a large-scale instance of a common laboratory phenomenon: the spark discharge. In this case, however, the research was not only productive, it was useful; it revealed the function of electricity in the "economy of nature" and it was applied by Franklin in an attempt to throw light on the whole process of cloud formation and rain.

But Franklin's research had led him to another conclusion, that a long vertical rod of metal, pointed at the top and set deep into the earth, would protect buildings from a stroke of lightning; the empirical test was to construct lightning rods in order to discover whether they would afford such protection (which Franklin, as an empiricist, never doubted), which is only another way of saying that the result of Franklin's research was a predicted new element of experience — a lightning rod — which had to be put to the trial of lightning.

This whole process of empirical science was beautifully described in the seventeenth century by Robert Hooke, who wrote:

So many are the links upon which the true philosophy depends, of which, if any one be loose, or weak, the whole chain is in danger of being dissolved; it is to begin with the hands and eyes, and to proceed on through the memory, to be continued by the reason; nor is it to stop there, but to come about to the hands and eyes again, and so, by a continual passage round from one faculty to another, it is to be maintained in life and strength, as much as the body of man is by the circulation of the blood through the several parts of the body. . . .

This is the sense in which Franklin's scientific research was productive and useful and fruitful. It was productive in that it led to a new theory of electrical action which was the source of a more profound understanding of nature, one which enabled men to predict (and for the first time) what would happen in many of their common electrical experiments in the laboratory, and it also led to many new physical phenomena that had never before been observed. It was useful in that it produced an instrument that enabled men (again for the first time) to protect their homes, barns, churches and ships from destruction by lightning. And the rod itself was fruitful in that it became an instrument that in Franklin's hands and ours has led to a deeper knowledge of the electrification of clouds and of the earth itself and the mechanism of the lightning discharge.

The doctrine of empiricism was always hospitable to the view of Bacon that "fruits and works" are "sponsors and sureties" for the truths of science. But we must keep in mind that Bacon had added that "works themselves are of greater value as pledges of truth than as contributing to the comforts of life." As an empirical scientist Franklin would have agreed, although, being Franklin, he might have questioned the word "greater." The empirical view of the scientist would be satisfied equally by the production of new experience, whether a phenomenon of importance or a device that embodied the newly discovered principles.

Franklin did not pursue the science of electricity because of a particular practical aim; had this been his intent he would hardly have chosen electricity as his major area of inquiry: in his day electricity was not a practical subject. The only supposedly practical application of electricity then was in a kind of medical therapy, but Franklin was convinced that the "cures" arose from the patient's desire to get well rather than from the electric shock. But once Franklin had reached the stage in his investigations where the new knowledge could be put to use in the service of man, he was quick to see an application. I believe that Franklin was convinced that pure science would always produce useful innovations, and here we may see him in the great scientific tradition that has only recently become a major feature of American civilization.

Throughout the nineteenth century, America was noted more for the applications of scientific discoveries that had been made in other lands than for the production of that fundamental scientific knowledge we applied so fruitfully. It is only in the last fifty years or so that America has risen to be a foremost scientific nation of the world. During the nineteenth century Franklin was considered by Americans to be an "applied scientist," the inventor of the lightning rod and the Franklin stove, and his whole contribution to pure science was reduced to the kite experiment. The great laboratory discoveries, the first unitary theory of electrical action — the research in pure science that made his contemporaries call him the Newton of their age — were ignored.

Today we are beginning to recognize that the applications of scientific discovery to the cure of disease, the improve-

ment of our living conditions and the safeguarding of our national existence must depend on fundamental discoveries to apply. We may, therefore, in this new tradition look back on Franklin as our first scientist. We may see him as one of those pioneers who understood that empirical science must *always* produce new experience which enlarges our view of nature and our understanding of the processes going on in the world around us, and that it *sometimes* produces (along the way) practical innovations of inestimable value for our health and our economic security. Characteristically, Franklin's most eloquent defense of that research in science that has no particular practical consequence in view took the form of a witticism. Watching the first balloon ascent in Paris, he overheard the usual question: What good is it? His reply has never been equaled: "What good is a newborn baby?" Discussing the new element chlorine, discovered in 1810, and applied to the bleaching of cloth, Michael Faraday said in 1816:

Before leaving this substance, chlorine, I will point out its history, as an answer to those who are in the habit of saying to every new fact, "What is its use?" Dr. Franklin says to such, "What is the use of an infant?" The answer of the experimentalist would be, "Endeavor to make it useful." When Scheele discovered this substance it appeared to have no use, it was in its infantine and useless state; but having grown up to maturity, witness its powers, and see what endeavors to make it useful have done.

Franklin's scientific ideas and his conception of the potentialities of science have influenced Americans only indirectly, through the nineteenth-century European masters under whom our scientists studied. But, wholly apart from his personal influence or the effect of his discoveries and theories on the development of science as such, his empirical approach to the world of man produced qualities of concept and action that are embodied in great American institutions and that have become a precious American heritage.

Franklin was not a true philosopher in the sense that Jonathan Edwards was, but he was a natural philosopher – in that larger sense in which scientific learning and a general outlook on God, man, nature and the world were included within a single expression in a day when scientists were not merely physicists or chemists or astronomers or biologists. Franklin may be fairly described as an empirical Newtonian in the realms of science and of human affairs. In both realms, the principles and conclusions of reason applied to experiential data – the facts of nature and the facts of man – had to be embodied in experience or they were meaningless and irrelevant. Franklin's understanding of nature led him to control nature's operations just as his knowledge of men's actions made him a master of men and the affairs of the world. And just as in science his conclusions became elements of experience in new phenomena to be observed or new instruments to be put in use, so in society new elements of experience were created and put to the trial of use: new institutions (a hospital, school and fire company), new rules of conduct, a new form of government, a tax, or a simple act of kindness.

It is well known that the original rough draft of the Declaration of Independence contained Jefferson's statement that principles such as that all men are created equal were held to be "sacred and undeniable," and that in the manuscript these words are changed in Franklin's handwriting to make the statement read: "We hold these principles to be self-

evident." Now historians usually interpret this alteration simply as a literary improvement and certainly Franklin's cadence has a wonderful ring to it and is much more effective than Jefferson's. But the difference between the two phrases is much more profound than mere literary quality. Jefferson implied that the principles in question were holy, of divine origin, and were to be respected and guarded with reverence for that reason: to deny them would be sacrilege. But "self-evident" was a technical or scientific term applied to axioms, as John Harris' popular eighteenth-century *Dictionary of Arts and Sciences* defined it, and was exemplified in such propositions as: "That nothing can act where it is not; That a thing cannot be and not be at the same time; That the whole is greater than a part; That where there is no law, there is no transgression; etc." Such an axiom is "a generally received ground principle or rule in any art or science," and "it cannot be made more plain and evident by demonstration, because 'tis its self much better known than any thing that can be brought to prove it." This is the sense in which Franklin's phrase represents the summit of effectiveness.

Axioms or postulates are considered in our contemporary scientific language (mathematics, logic) to be propositions which are assumed without proof solely for the purpose of exploring the consequences or logical deductions which follow from them. But in Newtonian science, consequences were deduced from axioms because the axioms were true, which should imply that if the reasoning process or deduction were correct, the results would be equally true or verifiable in experience. In the *Principia Mathematica* Newton explored the logical or mathematical consequences of certain laws of force, notably the famous three laws of motion and the law of universal gravitation. Now, as Newton explained the matter in 1713, "experimental philosophy" or empirical science "proceeds only from phenomena" or the data provided by experience, and it "deduces general propositions from them only by induction." Thus anyone who wanted to take exception to the *Principia* would have to "draw his objection from some experiment or phenomenon." In this "experimental philosophy," Newton added, the "first principles or axiomes which I call the laws of motion" are "deduced from phenomena and made general by induction: which is the highest evidence that a proposition can have in this philosophy."

In other words, Newton's scientific outlook in the *Principia Mathematica* was that the whole system of dynamics was derived by reason (*i.e.*, mathematics) from self-evident principles, which were "self-evident" because they were based on phenomena or experience; the test of the reasoning process and the correctness of interpretation of the evidence from which these principles were "deduced" (we would rather say "induced") lay in the conformity of the final results with phenomena or further experience.

Franklin's revision of the Declaration of Independence placed the principle that all men are created equal in the category of an axiom, self-evident; like the laws of motion, it was a principle "deduced" from experience. Now the particular experience that Franklin had in mind was probably his own and that of his fellow Americans. The inequalities in men's material circumstances or position that could be observed in Europe must have been a product of the artificial circumstances of society, continued by the system of class structure and hereditary rights. Proof lay in America, where land

was plentiful and where a man's fortune was apt to be determined by his industry, so that the differences between rich and poor tended to be less than in Europe. Franklin once compared American conditions to those in Ireland and Scotland, observing:

In those countries a small part of society are landlords, great noblemen, and gentlemen, extremely opulent, living in the highest affluence and magnificence; the bulk of the people tenants, living in the most sordid wretchedness in dirty hovels of mud and straw and clothed only in rags. I thought often of the happiness of New England, where every man is a freeholder, has a vote in public affairs, lives in a tidy, warm house, has plenty of good food and fuel, with whole clothes from head to foot, the manufacture perhaps of his own family. Long may they continue in this situation!

The absence of great differences between rich and poor in a land of opportunity, America, surely was empirical justification that such inequality was not a result of man's innate character. Of course, some men are better endowed than others, just as some men are more virtuous than others. As Poor Richard put the matter in "How to get riches"—"The art of getting riches consists very much in thrift. All men are not equally qualified for getting money, but it is in the power of every one alike to practise this virtue." This led to the conclusion that "Useful attainments in your minority will procure riches in maturity, of which writing and accounts are not the meanest." Hence the need for education: "Learning, whether speculative or practical, is, in popular or mixt governments, the natural source of wealth and honor."

We have already mentioned that Franklin was a confirmed abolitionist, but could he believe that Negroes were in any sense the equal of whites? Experience certainly showed that they were not, because anyone could observe that "negroes, who are free [and] live among the white people, . . . are generally improvident and poor." But experience must always be interpreted by reason, and in this case reason, said Franklin, tells us that free Negroes are not by nature "deficient in natural understanding," but simply that Negroes "have not the advantage of education." Here we may see more than an example of the application of reason to explain the data of experience, the condition of free Negroes. In considering society, ideas must be just as productive as in the study of nature. Thus Franklin's analysis was fruitful in creating a new form of experience, a trade school for Negroes, and by its means the whole doctrine was put to the test: if Negroes are inferior because they lack education, he said in effect, let us educate them and see whether they will not then be able to do the work of whites.

Franklin was secure in his convictions about the natural equality of men despite their color, and so he had no fear about the outcome of the proposed test in experience. As a matter of fact, Franklin firmly believed that truth could, by his definition, survive every experiential test which falsehood would necessarily fail; so it is very much in keeping with his character of empiricist that he maintained the freedom of the press, the right of the printer to publish all views and to let truth combat error publicly and vanquish her on the field of experience. Over and over we see Franklin embodying his conclusions in acts rather than concepts. It is misleading to think of him as the enemy of the abstract and master of the concrete, however, because this description would rob his empiricism of the role of reason. Reason produces concepts out of ex-

perience and these concepts are always abstract, like the mutually repelling invisible particles in the electric fluid which he supposed was transferred from one body to another in electrostatic experiments; or abstract generalizations about matter, like its inability to act where it is not, or about man, like equality or rights. But a wide gulf separated Franklin from those who professed equality, for example, but did not practice it universally. He was not necessarily more sincere than they were; he was motivated by a different philosophy which made each abstraction live in its productive effect upon society rather than live a life of its own. This may not be the dominant philosophy in our history, but Americans have often acted as if it were. Like Franklin we have worked to found and support schools, hospitals, orphanages, homes for the aged, and we too have tried to improve our cities and towns and generally to make our habitation on earth pleasanter.

Next to the scientist the businessman is probably the greatest empiricist the world knows. Dealing with facts and with figures, he too contrives theories and applies reason to the facts of experience. A businessman, be he a manufacturer, merchant or shopkeeper, who finds his theories killed by ugly facts will probably be a failure. To make money requires predictions about trends and events which are verified. To earn a fortune demands qualities of initiative, shrewdness, observation and judgment, but also an empirical temper of mind. Franklin's rise to fortune came from his industry and thrift, but also from his ability to see opportunities and to make the most of them and to gauge the public needs and desires.

Franklin's major contribution to political thought was a theory of population growth, based on the data available to him in America. He had observed that "the natural livelyhood of the thin inhabitants of a forest country is hunting; that of a greater number, pasturage; that of a middling population, agriculture; and that of the greatest, manufactures; which last must subsist the bulk of the people in a full country or they must be subsisted by charity, or perish." He claimed that the American population was increasing so as to double every twenty or twenty-five years and would continue to do so (it did up to about 1860) and that cheap and plentiful land, one of the principal causes of American population increase, would maintain high wages in America (as it did for at least a century).

Franklin's essay had two consequences. It influenced Malthus (in the second edition of his work) and it was embodied in action, in accordance with the empiricist philosophy. Franklin's observations on population growth produced his influential pamphlet advocating the annexing of Canada rather than Guadeloupe; America needed room for expansion. Furthermore, it led him to a view based on simple calculation that America would eventually become more populous than Britain. America in the 1750s and '60s was, he said, "to be considered as the frontier of the British empire," but in 1760 he wrote that he had "long been of opinion that the *foundations of the future grandeur and stability of the British empire lie in America;* and though, like other foundations, they are low and little seen, they are, nevertheless, broad and strong enough to support the greatest political structure human wisdom ever yet erected." Franklin's concern for the empire thus became, in a real sense, the interest of the future major partner. Franklin's political thinking was based always on his study of society — or societies — through history books he had read and firsthand observation.

The empirical scientist may wrestle with the facts revealed by his laboratory experiments, but as an empiricist he cannot deny them. Franklin's theory of electrical action was generally satisfactory even though it could not adequately explain the repulsion between two negatively charged bodies, and yet he could not deny that such repulsion existed — despite his theory. Experience, as every scientist knows, is a hard taskmaster and it often makes the investigator abandon or alter cherished ideas by presenting an ugly little fact that does not fit. Early in his electrical research, Franklin had such an experience and "observed a phenomenon or two" that he could not account for on the principles he had set forth. "In going on with these experiments," he commented, "how many pretty systems do we build, which we soon find ourselves obliged to destroy! If there is no other use discovered of electricity, this, however, is something considerable, that it may *help to make a vain man humble.*" This facing up to facts, so natural to scientists in their laboratories, was a valuable asset to Franklin in ordinary life. The *Autobiography* shows how easy it was for him to accept the realities of experience and to learn from them how to be effective in achieving his aims.

The inflexible facts of nature constantly remind the experimental scientist that he is human enough to err and they induce a kind of humility and honesty that are always concomitants of an empiricist outlook on nature, man or society. The successful investigator is familiar with the need of altering his most cherished theories to make them fit the realities of experiment, the only way in which he can save the phenomena without jeopardizing the fundamental axioms of his science. In many ways this quality of integrity and adaptability in the scientist reminds us of the statesman whose code permits him to effect a compromise on matters of detail and mechanism and even degree without sacrifice of his fundamental principles. Whether Franklin's outstanding performance as the representative of America in France during the Revolution arose from such qualities, or whether nothing more was required than a native shrewdness and the bargaining skill of a businessman, he was certainly a master of the conference table. His major contribution to the Constitution was that compromise between the large and small states on the question of representation in the Congress.

Carl Van Doren, Franklin's greatest biographer, has written that this compromise "was Franklin's great victory in the Convention." He was author of "the compromise which held the delegates together at a time when they were ready to break up without forming any new Federal agreement. The Constitution was not his document. But without the weight of his prestige and the influence of his temper there might have been no document at all."

One of the features of the Constitution that most appealed to Franklin was the provision for amendment on trial, the possibility for alterations to be made in the light of actual experience. I am convinced that in Franklin's mind the greatest experiment was not the test of the electrification of clouds but the test of whether a democratic form of government could be established in the world and whether it could survive the trials of experience and function as its framers had intended.

Carl Van Doren: CONCLUDING PAPER

DR. SIMON FLEXNER recently told me about his signing the Guest Book of the Royal Society. He asked to see Newton's autograph. So many before him had done this, and run their fingers beneath it as they read, that the name next after Newton's is completely wiped out. Dr. Flexner then turned to Franklin's name and found the name underneath his also worn away, though not quite so completely as the one under Newton's. Newton and Franklin were the only names so eminent as to have caused this obliteration of their neighbors.

But it must not be forgotten that Franklin, while a great scientist, was a great man of letters. He is no more to be judged merely by his "Autobiography" than Dr. Johnson is to be judged merely by "Rasselas" or the "Lives of the Poets." These men were greater writers than their books indicate. Their writings run through their lives.

Franklin said: "Prose writing has been of great value to me in my life, and was a principal means of my advancement." But he began by writing verse. His first Philadelphia friends, obscure youths who talked literature and philosophy as they walked along the Schuylkill with him, were all poets. It was with a poet, James Ralph, that Franklin first went to England. Franklin thought that writing verse was the best way of learning to write

From "Concluding Paper" by Carl Van Doren in *Meet Dr. Franklin* (Philadelphia: The Franklin Institute, 1943), pp. 227–234. Used by permission of the publishers.

prose, as it was. At twenty, when he sat down to write a scheme for the future conduct of his life, he had poetry in mind. He said: "Those who write of the art of poetry teach us that if we would write what may be worth reading we ought always, before we begin, to form a regular plan and design of our piece; otherwise we shall be in danger of incongruity. I am apt to think it is the same with life."

Thirty years later, writing to George Whitefield, Franklin used another poetical illustration: "Life, like a dramatic piece, should not only be conducted with regularity but methinks it should finish handsomely. Being now in the last act, I begin to cast about for something fit to end with. Or if mine be more properly compared with an epigram, as some of the lines are barely tolerable I am very desirous of concluding with a bright point."

Franklin in 1744 read Thomson's "Seasons" with tears of pleasure. In 1782 he read Cowper's poems, some of them twice over, "though," he said "the relish for reading of poetry had long left me." But Franklin's drinking songs are probably his best expressions in verse.

In his prose it is obvious that he went through a great deal of experimentation in different modes. Though I have now too little time for a full discussion of this I can illustrate it with certain passages which show his range of prose style.

For instance, here is a sharp realism in his "Reflections on Courtship and Marriage":

"Let us survey the morning dress of some women. Downstairs they come, pulling up their ungartered, dirty stockings; slipshod, with naked heels peeping out; no stays or other decent conveniency, but all flip-flop; a sort of a clout thrown about the neck, half on and half off, with the frowzy hair hanging in sweaty ringlets, staring like Medusa with her ser-

pents; shrugging up her petticoats, that are sweeping the ground and scarce tied on; hands unwashed, teeth furred, and eyes crusted — but I beg your pardon, I'll go no farther with this sluttish picture, which I am afraid has already turned your stomach."

If Franklin had put his mind to it he could have written as good novels as Fielding.

√ Here is the opening sentence of "Some Account of the Pennsylvania Hospital." Franklin, who had assisted Dr. Thomas Bond in the founding of the Hospital, as you know, was asked to write a history of it, which he published in 1754. His opening sentence is an example of homespun splendor hardly to be matched in the English language. The great sentences with which writers begin books commonly make use of flaming words; Franklin's words are all plain. His magic comes from his cadence and the emotion it implies.

"About the end of the year 1750 some persons who had frequent opportunities of observing the distress of such distempered poor as from time to time came to Philadelphia for the advice and assistance of the physicians and surgeons of that city; how difficult it was for them to procure suitable lodgings and other conveniences proper for their respective cases and how expensive the providing good and careful nurses and other attendants for want whereof many must suffer greatly, and some probably perish, that might otherwise have been restored to health and comfort and become useful to themselves, their families, and the public for many years after; and considering moreover that even the poor inhabitants of this city though they had homes were therein but badly accommodated in sickness and could not so well and easily be taken care of in their separate habitations as they might be in one convenient house, under one inspection and in the hands of skillful practitioners, and several of the inhabitants of the province who unhappily became disordered in their senses wandered about to the terror of their neighbors, there being no place (except the house of correction) in which they might be confined and subjected to proper management for their recovery, and that house was by no means fitted for such purposes; did charitably consult together and confer with their friends and acquaintances on the best means of relieving the distressed under those circumstances."

Franklin was perhaps most expert in his letters, always skillfully adapted to the circumstances or to the correspondents. Here is his grand style, as written to Washington in 1780, inviting Washington to come to Europe where Franklin was then minister to France:

"Should peace arrive after another campaign or two, and afford us a little leisure, I should be happy to see your Excellency in Europe and to accompany you, if my age and strength would permit, in visiting some of its ancient and most famous kingdoms. You would, at this side of the sea, enjoy the great reputation you have acquired, pure and free from those little shades that the jealousy of a man's countrymen and contemporaries are ever endeavoring to cast over living merit. Here you would enjoy, and know, what posterity will say of Washington. For a thousand leagues have nearly the same effect as a thousand years; the feeble voice of those grovelling passions cannot extend so far in either time or distance. At present I enjoy that pleasure for you, as I frequently hear the old generals of this martial country (who study the maps of America and mark upon them all your operations) speak with sincere approba-

tion and great applause of your conduct; and join in giving you the character of one of the great captains of the age.

"I must soon quit the scene, but you may live to see our country flourish, as it will amazingly and rapidly after the war is over; like a field of young Indian corn, which long fair weather and sunshine had enfeebled and discolored, and which, in that weak state, by a thunder-gust of violent wind, hail, and rain seemed to be threatened with absolute destruction; yet the storm being past, it recovers fresh verdure, shoots up with double vigor, and delights the eye not of its owner only but of every observing traveler."

Franklin's impish style appears in his famous model for a letter of introduction. He wrote it in Paris where he was asked for so many letters of introduction for people that he did not know. I doubt that he ever used this for an actual letter — but only thought he would like to. This is what he wrote:

"The bearer of this, who is going to America, presses me to give him a letter of introduction, though I know nothing of him, not even his name. This may seem extraordinary, but I assure you it is not uncommon here. Sometimes, indeed, one unknown person brings another, equally unknown, to recommend him; and sometimes they recommend one another. As to this gentleman, I must refer you to himself for his character and merits, with which he is certainly better acquainted than I can possibly be. I recommend him, however, to those civilities which every stranger of whom one knows no harm has a right to expect; and I request that you will do him all the good offices, and show him all the favor, that on further acquaintance you shall find him to deserve."

For Franklin letters were long-distance conversation. He wrote hundreds not only perfectly expressive of his own meanings but also delicately adapted to the recipients, whether children, elegant ladies, scientists, or politicians. Letters to him were a form of art. And they might be a relief, as in the famous letter to Strahan 5 July 1775, which Franklin wrote as a poet might have written a poem: to clear his mind and heart.

Franklin's method in writing was described by him in the last year of his life, in a letter of advice to Benjamin Vaughan:

"Before you sit down to write on any subject . . . spend some days in considering it, putting down at the same time, in short hints, every thought which occurs to you as proper to make a part of your intended piece. When you have thus obtained a collection of the thoughts, examine them carefully with this view, to find which of them is properest to be presented first to the mind of the reader, that he, being possessed of that, may the more easily understand it, and be disposed to receive what you intend for the second; and thus I would have you put a figure before each thought, to mark its future place in your composition. For so, every preceding proposition preparing the mind for that which is to follow, and the reader often anticipating it, he proceeds with ease, and pleasure, and approbation, as seeming continually to meet with his own thoughts. In this mode you have better chance for a perfect production; because, the mind attending first to the sentiments alone, next to the method alone, each part is likely to be better performed, and I think too in less time."

There are many revisions in his manuscripts. He wrote prose as careful poets write poetry. It is interesting to note certain changes he made in the text of his last speech before the Constitutional Convention, as revealed in the manuscript version in the Library of Cornell University. Franklin originally wrote: "I must own that there were several parts of this Constitution which I do not at present approve." He thought again, apparently, and certainly reduced the sentence of eighteen words to eleven: "I confess that I do not entirely approve of this Constitution." Or again, he wrote that he had often in his long life found himself obliged "to change opinions . . . which I once thought right but found to be wrong." The antithesis was too blunt, so he changed it to read: "which I once thought right but found to be otherwise." Cadence with Franklin was very important. In yet another passage he had spoken of the prejudices, passions, errors of opinion, local interests, and selfish views of any assembly of men. He first wrote: "From the fermentation of this heterogeneous mixture can a perfect production be expected?" He struck out "the fermentation of this heterogeneous mixture" and substituted simply "from such an assembly." The simplifying change reminds us of change in the Declaration where Jefferson had written: "We hold these truths to be sacred and undeniable." Franklin — for the writing seems clearly to be his — changed "sacred and undeniable" to "self-evident."

I need hardly speak of the "Autobiography." . . . But I should like again to call attention to the fact that Rousseau and Franklin together, at almost the same time, struck out all the essential lines the autobiography as a literary form was to take after them. Franklin's "Autobiography" is so familiar and so intimate that we hardly think of it as a book. It simply exists.

So with his masterly Poor Richard sayings. I have pointed out more than once that the economical maxims make up a smaller share of Poor Richard's wisdom than is commonly realized. They were collected partly for dramatic effect, in the long preface to the almanac for 1758 and were at once — and ever since — separately reprinted, whereas the others have been more or less buried in the rare original files. In a small volume in the inexpensive Pocket Books series, issued in 1940 on the 150th anniversary of Franklin's death, I selected, along with the "Autobiography" and minor writings, a hundred or so of the maxims of Poor Richard on the many topics he touched. (This selection has since then been translated into Spanish and published in Mexico, the first volume in a new series of reprints initiated there in 1942.)

Here are some sayings of Poor Richard which must be taken into account if the full range of Franklin as aphorist is to be comprehended. "Thou hadst better eat salt with the philosophers of Greece than sugar with the courtiers of Italy." "The brave and the wise can both pity and excuse when cowards and fools show no mercy." "As charms are nonsense, nonsense is a charm." "Avarice and happiness never saw each other. How then should they become acquainted?" "Sloth and silence are a fool's virtues." "Hast thou virtue? Acquire also the graces and beauties of virtue." "If you would not be forgotten, as soon as you are dead and rotten, either write things worth reading, or do things worth the writing." "He that falls in love with himself will have no rivals." "Sin is not hurtful because it is forbidden, but it is forbidden because it is hurtful." "What's proper is becoming. See the blacksmith with his white silk apron." Others are:

"The most exquisite folly is made of wisdom spun too fine." "We are not so sensible of the greatest health as of the least sickness." "He that is secure is not safe." "He is not well bred that cannot bear ill breeding in others." "Having been poor is no shame, but being ashamed of it is." "Cunning proceeds from want of capacity." "'Tis against some men's principle to pay interest, and seems against others' interest to pay the principal." "If you would be loved, love and be lovable." "It is ill manners to silence a fool, and cruelty to let him go on." "Half a truth is often a great lie."

Of course Franklin drew his proverbs from many sources, but he almost always improved both the flavor and the cadence. For example, William Herbert in 1640 quoted: "Bells call others, but themselves enter not into the church." Franklin says: "The bell calls others to church, but itself never minds the sermon." Herbert said: "Help thyself, and God will help thee." Franklin: "God helps them that help themselves."

Franklin's sayings are likely to have graphic images and racy words. One of his sayings he tried three times. In 1740 he wrote "An empty bag cannot stand upright." In 1750: "An empty sack can hardly stand upright; but if it does, 'tis a stout one." In 1758: "'Tis hard for an empty bag to stand upright" — the final form. A good instance of his way with an older proverb is to be found in what he did with the Scottish: "Fat housekeepers make lean executors." Franklin made it: "A fat kitchen, a lean will."

There is one saying first noted in 1572: "A gloved cat can catch no mice"; in 1611: "Cuffed cat's no good mouse-hunt"; in 1629: "A muzzled cat was never good mouser"; in 1641: "A gloved cat was never a good hunter"; in 1670: "A muffled cat is no good mouser." Then Franklin in 1754: "The cat in gloves catches no mice." To a sensitive ear the improvement in cadence is instant and irresistible.

Another one: Plautus in one of his plays said that no guest is welcome after three days. Lyly in "Euphues" made it: "Fish

and guests in three days are stale."
Sancho Panza in "Don Quixote" agreed
with him. In 1670 the proverb appeared
in an English collection as: "Fresh fish
and new come guests, smell by they are
three days old." A Scottish collection in
1721 gave it as: "Fresh fish and poor
friends become soon ill sar'd" — ill sa-
vored. Then Franklin in 1736: "Fish and
visitors stink in three days." The whole
philosophy of the weekend.

Franklin's sayings are sometimes
homely and rustic, as he meant them to
be. His language belonged to the future
because it had a simplicity and clarity
that are timeless. If his sayings could
travel backward in time instead of forward, they would probably seem as clear
to his ancestors as they do to his descendants.

Franklin was first of all a great man,
who was great in many ways. As he held
few high offices, and made almost no
speeches, he had to depend — and chose
to depend — chiefly on writing as his

means of making himself felt in the world.
He had no Boswell to perpetuate his conversation. Franklin survives, directly or
indirectly, in the written and remembered
words he left behind him. The legendary
Franklin comes, with some distortion,
from the autobiographical Franklin, who
was explicit and candid about himself, so
far as he took the trouble to tell his story.

Parson Weems could turn Washington
into a legend, but Weems, though he
wrote a life of Franklin, could not compete with Franklin's "Autobiography," the
most widely read autobiography in the
world. And in it and elsewhere Franklin
is unique in English. No other writer in
the language so perfectly combines "a
felicitous elegance with a happy vernacu-
lar," the grace of art and the wit of nature.
He had countless things to say, and never
said one of them badly. A critic who
thinks Franklin is not a great man of letters simply does not know what a man of
letters is.

Suggestions for Additional Reading

A very good early biography of Franklin which aimed at rescuing him from the myth-making processes and idealizations of the nineteenth century is George S. Fisher's *The True Benjamin Franklin* (Philadelphia, 1899, reprinted in 1926). The best recent one-volume studies are Carl Van Doren's *Benjamin Franklin* (New York, 1938) and Verner W. Crane's *Benjamin Franklin and a Rising People* (Boston, 1954). Carl Becker wrote a brilliantly concise sketch for the *Dictionary of American Biography* (VI, 1931) which was reprinted by the Cornell University Press in 1946. A useful collection of essays by leading Franklin authorities appears in *Meet Dr. Franklin* (Philadelphia, 1943).

The ardent seeker for the truth about Franklin and his relationship to American society will not be satisfied with the brief selections from Franklin's own writings included in this volume. A minimal reading assignment in the original sources should be the complete *Autobiography,* of which there are numerous trustworthy editions in print. The cheapest and most accessible of these are the Rinehart edition edited by Dixon Wecter, the Modern Library edition edited by Henry Steele Commager, and the edition edited by Herbert W. Schneider for the Liberal Arts Press. For the more scholarly student Max Farrand has prepared a corrected, variorum edition (Berkeley, 1949). Since Franklin does not paint the most flattering picture of himself in the *Autobiography,* one should also consult his other writings. The standard edition of his collected works remains *The Writings of Benjamin Franklin,* edited by Albert H. Smyth (New York, 1905–1907), 10 volumes. A comprehensive anniversary edition of the Franklin papers is currently being prepared by Yale University and the American Philosophical Society. If his collected works are not available, generous selections from his writing can be found in Carl Van Doren, ed., *Benjamin Franklin and Jonathan Edwards: Selections from Their Writings* (New York, 1920); Carl Van Doren, ed., *Benjamin Franklin's Autobiographical Writings* (New York, 1945); Frank L. Mott and Chester E. Jorgenson, eds., *Benjamin Franklin: Representative Selections, with Introduction, Bibliography, and Notes,* American Writers Series (New York, 1936); Nathan G. Goodman, ed., *A Benjamin Franklin Reader* (New York, 1945); and I. Bernard Cohen, ed., *Benjamin Franklin: His Contribution to the American Tradition,* Makers of the American Tradition Series (New York and Indianapolis, 1953). The last, as its sub-title suggests, is particularly useful in connection with the problem posed in this volume.

In order to be able to define and assess what is original about Franklin's contributions to American life one should also know something about the eighteenth-century environment which produced him. For this purpose the biographies listed above are, of course, helpful. Good general studies of the colonial background are Herbert L. Osgood, *The American Colonies in the Eighteenth Century* (New York, 1924), 4 volumes, and Curtis P. Nettels, *The Roots of American Civilization* (New York, 1938). A more sharply focused study emphasizing the urban influence on Franklin is Carl and Jessica Bridenbaugh, *Rebels and Gentlemen: Philadelphia in the Age of Franklin* (New York, 1942). Useful in countering this emphasis is Frederick J. Turner, *The Frontier in American History* (New York, 1920), chapters I–III; and Gilbert Chinard, "Looking Westward," in *Meet Dr. Franklin*, 135–150. Clinton Rossiter relates Franklin to the political climate of opinion in his *Seedtime of the Republic: the Origin of the American Tradition of Political Liberty* (New York, 1953), 281–312. The key ideas of the European Enlightenment, also current in America, are brilliantly analyzed by Carl Becker in *The Heavenly City of the Eighteenth-Century Philosophers* (New Haven, 1932). The intellectual content of American Puritanism is best attained through the introductions and selections found in Perry Miller and Thomas H. Johnson, eds., *The Puritans* (New York, 1938).

The problem, or problems, posed in this volume grow out of the history of Franklin's reputation and are largely concerned with moral and social values. A useful aid in discovering the history of Franklin's reputation is Charles W. Moulton, ed., *The Library of Literary Criticism of English and American Authors*, IV (Buffalo, 1902). J. H. Smythe, Jr., ed., *The Amazing Benjamin Franklin* (New York, 1929) is an anthology of brief popular estimates not readily available elsewhere. An excellent guide to Franklin mythology is Dixon Wecter's chapter on Franklin in *The Hero in America: A Chronicle of Hero-Worship* (New York, 1941). Louis B. Wright's article, "Franklin's Legacy to the Gilded Age," *Virginia Quarterly Review*, XXII (1946), 268–279, amply demonstrates the lasting influence of "Poor Richard." I. Bernard Cohen is particularly concerned

with the role of Franklin in the formation of the national character in his lengthy introduction to *Benjamin Franklin: His Contribution to the American Tradition*, listed above. The concept of "national character" itself introduces a knotty problem which is discussed by Margaret Mead in her article on that subject in A. L. Kroeber, Chairman, *Anthropology Today: An Encyclopedic Inventory* (Chicago, 1953), 642–667.

It has been popular to claim Franklin as a representative and molder of the American character. To the extent that one accepts this claim, what one thinks of Franklin and his influence depends largely on how one interprets the national character and how well disposed he feels toward it. In the final analysis, when all the facts are in, after the specialized studies on Franklin as economist, general, postmaster, diplomat, etc., have been read, we resort to the realm of values. These monographs on different aspects of the "many-sided" Franklin can be located in the bibliographies of many of the works listed above. A distinguished recent monograph not yet committed to bibliographies is Gerald Stourzh, *Benjamin Franklin and American Foreign Policy* (Chicago, 1954). But it is the over-all evaluation of Franklin with which this volume is concerned. Some of the more penetrating and stimulating appreciations are Paul Elmer More, "Franklin," in his *Shelburne Essays*, Fourth Series (New York, 1906), 129–155; Theodore Parker, "Benjamin Franklin," in his *Historic Americans* (Boston, 1908, written in 1858); Vernon L. Parrington, "Benjamin Franklin," in *Main Currents in American Thought*, I (New York, 1927), 164–178; C. A. Saint-Beuve, "Franklin," in his *Portraits of the Eighteenth Century*, trans. K. P. Wormeley (New York, 1905),

I, 311–375; the entire chapter on Franklin in William Stebbing, *Some Verdicts of History Reviewed* (London, 1887); and H. T. Tuckerman, "Benjamin Franklin, the American Philosopher," in his *Biographical Essays* (Boston, 1857), 456–475. Parker and Tuckerman reflect the views of American Transcendentalism both in its admiration of Franklin and in its rather minor reservations. Stebbing and Saint-Beuve present English and Continental viewpoints. Finally, Max Farrand in his "Self-Portraiture: The Autobiography," in *Meet Dr. Franklin* (listed above) defends Franklin against the acrimonious onslaught of Charles Angoff which is included in this volume.

Good, trenchant criticism of Franklin is more difficult to come by, for the tendency has been to condemn Franklin before all the facts are in or in spite of the facts. The chief charge against Franklin, and perhaps the most defensible — his materialism — takes a variety of different forms. A favorite device has been to juxtapose Franklin's values with those of another admired American, allowing the reader to draw his own conclusions, presumably, to the prejudice of Franklin. The polarity between Franklin and his contemporary Jonathan Edwards seems to have been most popular. The best contrast of Franklin and Edwards, too long for inclusion in this volume, is that of Kenneth B. Murdock in Arthur H. Quinn, ed., *The Literature of the American People: An Historical and Critical Survey* (New York, 1951), 106–123. Unlike Professor Davidson, whose very similar essay appears in this volume, Professor Murdock concludes that America is fortunate in having both Franklin and Edwards. Josephine Herbst, *New Green World* (New York, 1954), 93–94, contrasts Franklin with John and William Bartram,

eighteenth-century poet-naturalists. The book which led A. Whitney Griswold to his comparison of the economic views of Franklin and Cotton Mather, reprinted here, and which gave an additional fillip to attacks on Franklin's bourgeois character is Max Weber, *The Protestant Ethic and the Spirit of Capitalism,* trans. Talcott Parsons (London, 1930). A somewhat inadequate rebuttal of Weber's thesis in so far as it applies to Franklin and the American scene is found in Samuel E. Morison, *Builders of the Bay Colony* (Boston, 1930), 160–169. John Dos Passos contrasts the eighteenth-century careers of Franklin and Daniel Defoe in the *New Republic,* CIII (1940), 654–657, 689–691, in order to prove the superiority of the American way of life.

A group most consistently critical of Franklin has been the creative writers and poets. The essays of D. H. Lawrence and Charles Angoff in this volume can be supplemented by Joseph Dennie, "On Franklin," in *The Port Folio* for 1803, reprinted in Edwin H. Cady, ed., *Literature of the Early Republic* (Rinehart, 1950), 477–481; Nathaniel Hawthorne, "Benjamin Franklin; A Biographical Story," *Works* (Boston, 1884), XII, 189–202; Herman Melville's fictionalized characterization in *Israel Potter* (London, 1923); Mark Twain, "The Late Benjamin Franklin," *Writings* (National Edition), XIX, 211–215; and especially William Carlos Williams, "Poor Richard," in *In the American Grain* (Norfolk, Conn., 1925), 144–157. The impressionistic rendering by William Carlos Williams parallels the D. H. Lawrence essay in this volume both in style and point of view. Josephine Herbst in her book, already mentioned in another category, seems to follow the lead of William Carlos Williams. An amusing reversal of the pattern of hero-worship established in children's literature is Robert Lawson, *Ben and Me: An Astonishing Life of Benjamin Franklin, By His Good Mouse Amos* (Boston, 1945).

If further aids are desirable in grappling with this problem on Franklin, consult the bibliographies in Frank L. Mott and Chester E. Jorgenson, eds., *Benjamin Franklin: Representative Selections* (see above); R. E. Spiller, *et al, Literary History of the United States,* III (New York, 1949); and Paul L. Ford, *Franklin Bibliography: A List of Books Written by or Relating to Benjamin Franklin* (Brooklyn, N. Y., 1889).